Aliza Nisenbaum

Taking Care

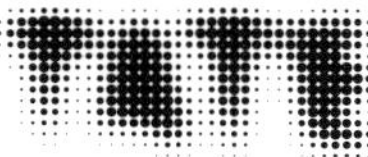

I would like to thank all those who let me paint them
and who took the time to share their stories:

Leanne Binns
Leah Bradley
Jessica Dawber
Sue Dewsbury
Charlotte Durand
Alan Fitzpatrick
Rose Floyd
Kevin Henderson
Emily Johnson
Claire Jones
Colin Jones
Sarah Jones
Shirley Mulvaney
Jackie Parry
Jo Potier de la Morandiere
Ryan Edwin Robinson
Calum Semple
Stephen Smith
Shari Soriano
Ann Taylor
Naveena Tom
Amanda Turton
Jodie Walton
Lalith Wijedoru
Tracey Wileman

And I am grateful to Dan Bentley for photographing
all the sitters, allowing me to work remotely.

For making the commission and exhibition a success,
I would like to thank everyone at Tate Liverpool,
with a special mention to Helen Legg; Tamar Hemmes;
Tom Emery; Jenny Hunter and the Art Handling team;
Denise Courcoux; Jennifer Collingwood; Dominic Beaumont;
Laura Irving and the Visitor Experience team.

I'd like to express my gratitude also to Tom Avery, Emilia Will
and Bill Jones from the Tate Publishing team for making
this publication a reality. And all credit to Lorenz Klingebiel
for his beautiful design of the book.

Many thanks as well to Anton Kern, Brigitte Mulholland,
Christoph Gerozissis and Erin Harris at Anton Kern Gallery
for their ongoing support.

Contents

Aliza Nisenbaum at Tate Liverpool

TAMAR HEMMES

Known for her vibrant and intimate paintings, Aliza Nisenbaum creates portraits that focus on different community groups. Previously, she has collaborated with undocumented immigrants, London Underground staff and museum security guards. She believes that 'paying attention can be a political act' and usually spends hours with her sitters, painting them from life while developing a personal connection through conversations that enable her to capture their individuality.

We initially invited Nisenbaum to join us at Tate Liverpool for a residency in Spring/Summer 2020, during which she planned to work with people who had created their own communities around local allotments. The global health crisis soon highlighted the incredible dedication of key workers and the lack of recognition given to many working in the public sector. Following an open call for applications to take part in the project, Nisenbaum decided to focus her attention on NHS staff from the Merseyside region whose work has proven vital during the Covid-19 pandemic.

Over four months, Nisenbaum painted two large-scale group portraits, depicting a team from Alder Hey Children's Hospital and eleven individual watercolour paintings of staff from Wirral University Teaching Hospital and The Royal Liverpool Hospital, and student nurses from Edge Hill University. The people portrayed in these new works represent a broad range of care workers, including doctors, nurses, porters, researchers and healthcare assistants. They are shown alongside things that have given them support and hope through this difficult time, highlighting the impact that Covid-19 has had on their work and home lives. The exhibition and this publication include the powerful and at times emotional stories of all those who posed for Nisenbaum, written in their own words.

'Aliza Nisenbaum – Painting the NHS',
film still (below and overleaf)

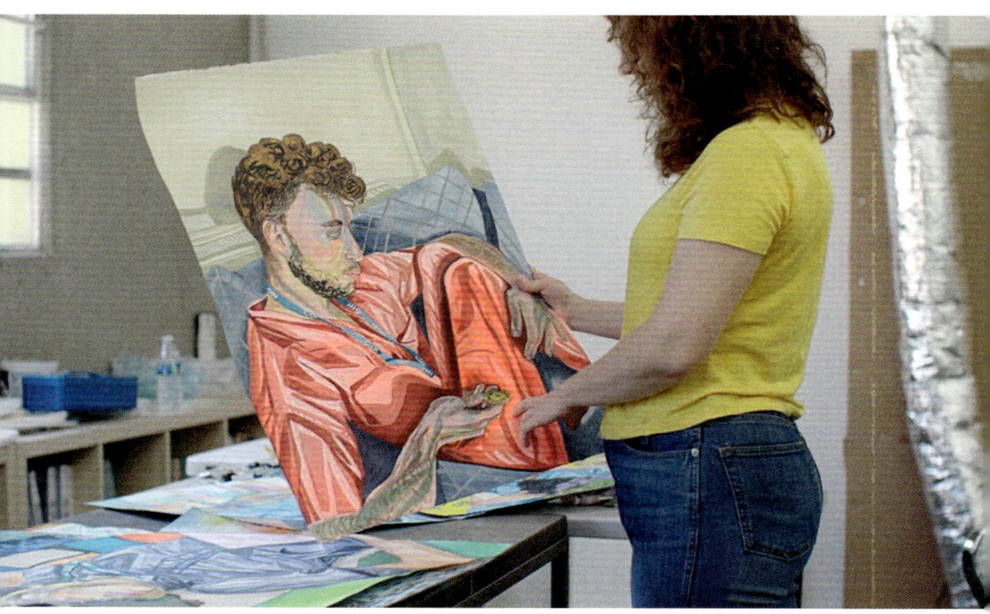

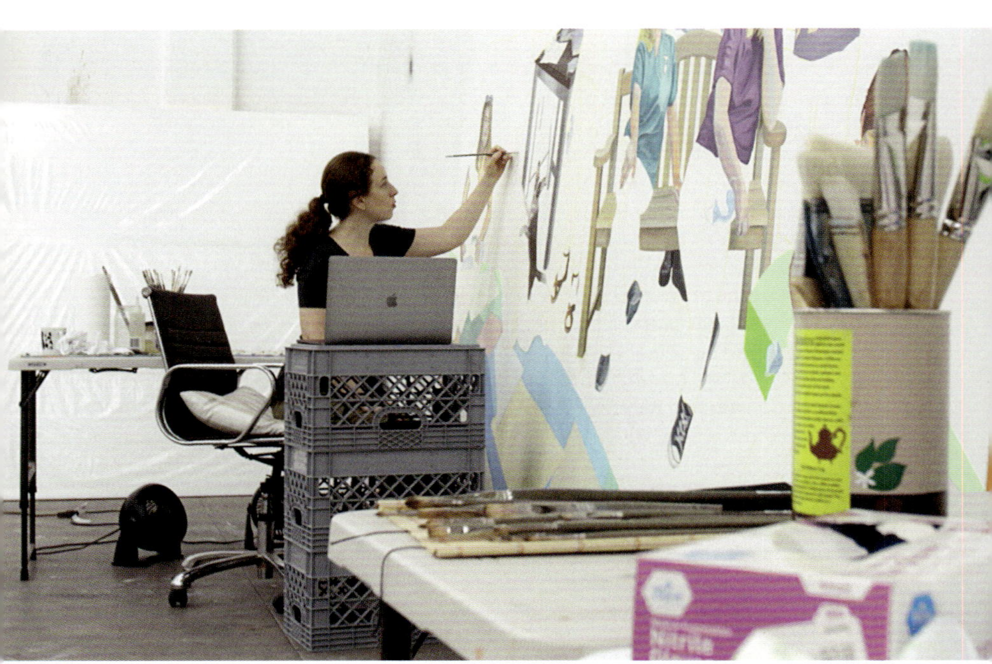

Painting the NHS

Artist ALIZA NISENBAUM speaks to curator
TAMAR HEMMES about her exhibition at
Tate Liverpool and the process of creating
new works during the Covid-19 pandemic

TAMAR HEMMES
Aliza, you've spoken before about how you were influenced by artists like Sylvia Sleigh, Alice Neel, and María Izquierdo, especially their depictions of private moments and the way that they express vulnerability. The conversations you had with your sitters as part of this project brought up some quite personal and emotional stories. I think it became clear early on that it was important to find a balance between highlighting the impacts of the pandemic on their professional but also personal lives. How did you approach this responsibility of telling the stories of NHS staff?

ALIZA NISENBAUM
I really love Sylvia Sleigh. María Izquierdo and Alice Neel were also perceptive when depicting character, attentively capturing the vulnerability of their subjects. Even though my work is often large in scale, portraying groups, it's made up of individual sittings witnessing each person, as well as the peer relationships of a workplace. In this instance, I was interested in painting a portrait where a person might be lost in their own thoughts, even if one is performing a very public task in one's profession. I liked the challenge of thinking about how to make a painting that shows the relationship between the private and public – discreet moments where people find renewal to go out and do their demanding jobs.

There was so little known about the virus in the early stages, therefore healthcare workers found that their work was overlapping with their personal lives in ways that they might not have experienced before – like so many having to isolate from their families. Shirley had to isolate from her children in her own home, not being able to show them physical affection, while working long shifts, packing around six months of simulation training into a few weeks.

Alan's story was particularly poignant – his mother passed away right as he was completing his nursing degree. Yet he started his NHS placement, the final element of his degree, with the knowledge that his mum would have been proud. Alan and I really connected when we spoke. He told me he loves art, cooking and dancing. He was interested in the fact I had painted dancers before. In some ways he reminds me of the dancers I've painted, because of his elegance – and yet his Covid story became a balancing act between this very tragic situation with his mother and working on the front lines during the pandemic.

Calum has worked on pandemic preparedness since 2011 and is part of ISARIC (International Severe Acute Respiratory and Emerging Infection Consortium) and SAGE (Scientific Advisory Group for Emergencies). Because of all the work they did, they were able to rapidly begin treatment and vaccine research. They were really heroes. Yet many people did not want to face reality. At times he said he was made to feel like a villain because of sceptics, or those who blamed the downturn of the economy on their efforts.

There's a real intimacy to your work because of these personal stories, but also because it's a very close examination of someone's physicality – the colours of their skin and the different features that make someone unique. Normally you spend hours with sitters in the same space, painting them from life, but for these portraits you had to rely on photographs, and on creating

**a virtual connection through Zoom.
I can imagine that in a way this added
a layer of intimacy, because you were
invited into people's homes.**

There's a lot to be said for the presence
and physicality of a breathing human
being when they're sitting right in front
of you to be painted; that gives me a lot
of energy. This time being at a remove
and having to meet people through Zoom
provided space for reflection and a different layer of intimacy. Many of them would
follow up these calls with more pictures
from their homes and images of their
uniforms, extending the time to stage
the paintings and reflect on their person-
alities. I'm grateful to Dan Bentley, the
photographer who worked with me on
site in Liverpool, as he went to people's
homes and to the hospital and gave
me lots of source material to work with.

I would never in a million years
imagine that I would get to see so many
homes of healthcare workers. It's an
insight into the lives of such public-fac-
ing individuals that's rare to experience.
Calum, for example, is a highly skilled
professor at the forefront of research
to beat the virus, yet he was excited
to give me a tour of his home and show
me the paintings made by the Scottish
Colourists he owns. Jessica told me
all about her grandmother, who was
a great influence on her and loved art.
We decided to use the hopscotch rug
created from jumpers her grandmother
had made as the background of her
portrait. Ann chose a pose with her
face resting on her hand that she later
recalled was a pose her mother used
to assume. She told me that she swears
like a docker, but it was also very clear
that she has great love for her patients
and her work in addiction. To me, Ann's
portrait captures this pride in her work.

**Another element of your work that
really stands out to me is the layering
of paint and the use of very vibrant
colours that are not ordinarily used
to represent different skin tones.
Could you speak about the meaning
of colour in your work?**

Colour is really my favourite part of
painting, because it's like an endless
puzzle to be resolved. It's almost like
smell in the way it bypasses the brain
and goes straight to our memories and
our feelings. I grew up in Mexico City,
in a house full of colour and pattern,
and my colour choices unconsciously
reflect this background.

When I'm painting somebody
from life, I try to pay attention to the
nuances of their skin. Colour is hugely
contingent, it's so much about light
and mood. No skin tone is alike, and
to me it's a metaphor for how multi-
faceted our identities actually are.
I try to really push my colour choices,
with sometimes slightly dissonant
combinations, or things that might
be unusual. In the big Alder Hey
painting I decided to put a very bright
yellow sun because I was living in
Los Angeles and I thought, 'I'll add
a bit of California sunshine as a way
of sending good vibes to Liverpool'.

Lalith was really taken by the huge
range of colours – he said, 'They're the
colours of the rainbow that you chose
for my face!'. I met him and Jo over
Zoom to show them the final outcome
of the painting, and he told Jo, 'Aliza
made you look like a movie star!'. We
had a good laugh about that. It wasn't
as quick a feedback loop as I usually
have when I'm painting someone from
life. Frankly, I breathed a sigh of relief
when I heard they were pleased with
the outcome of their portraits.

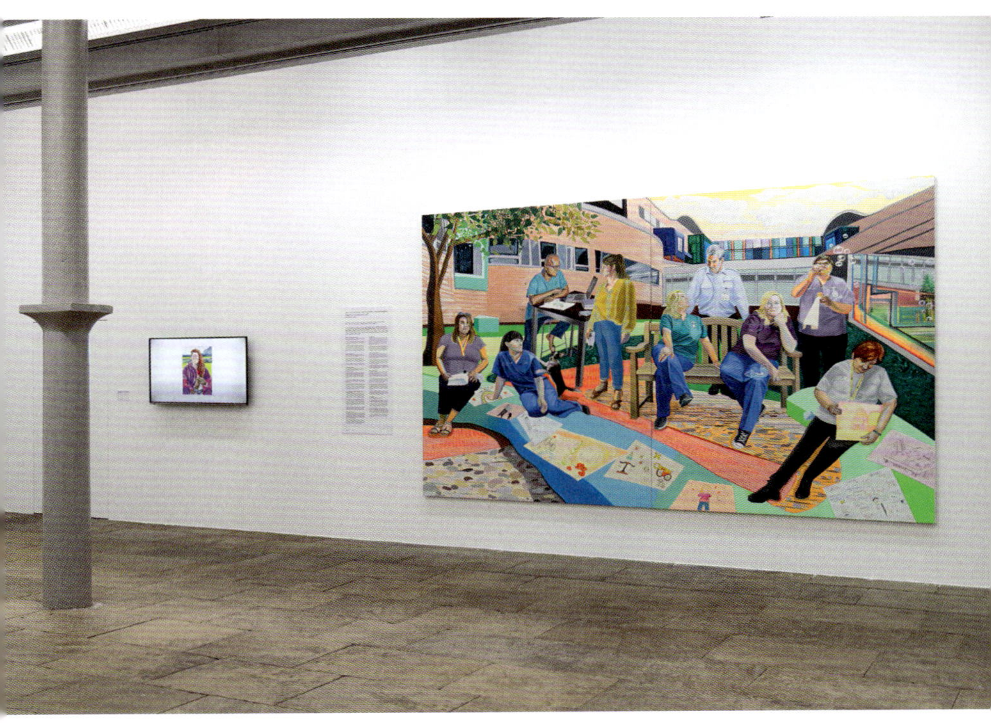

Installation shot of the exhibition at Tate Liverpool

One of the things that you've said is that the way that you paint is a 'cumulative register of time spent with someone', which I think is a really beautiful way to describe your process. For these new works, as we've said, there was less contact between you and your sitters because you worked remotely, and I can imagine that required a different approach as well. You didn't have the initial feedback from the sitters, so you had more time to reflect on your interactions. Do you feel that changed the outcome?

Painting is both an image and an accumulation of various events – its durational. Your own mood, the speed of your gestures, and ultimately how you respond to another person shape the final portrait.

The start of the pandemic was such a tough time for all of us – I questioned how to pay tribute and do justice to honour these people who are putting their lives on the line. And it gave me a real sense of purpose during the pandemic.

The paintings depict the outcome of all the back-and-forth between the sitters and I to come up with a composition and the poses, the story of their lives and how

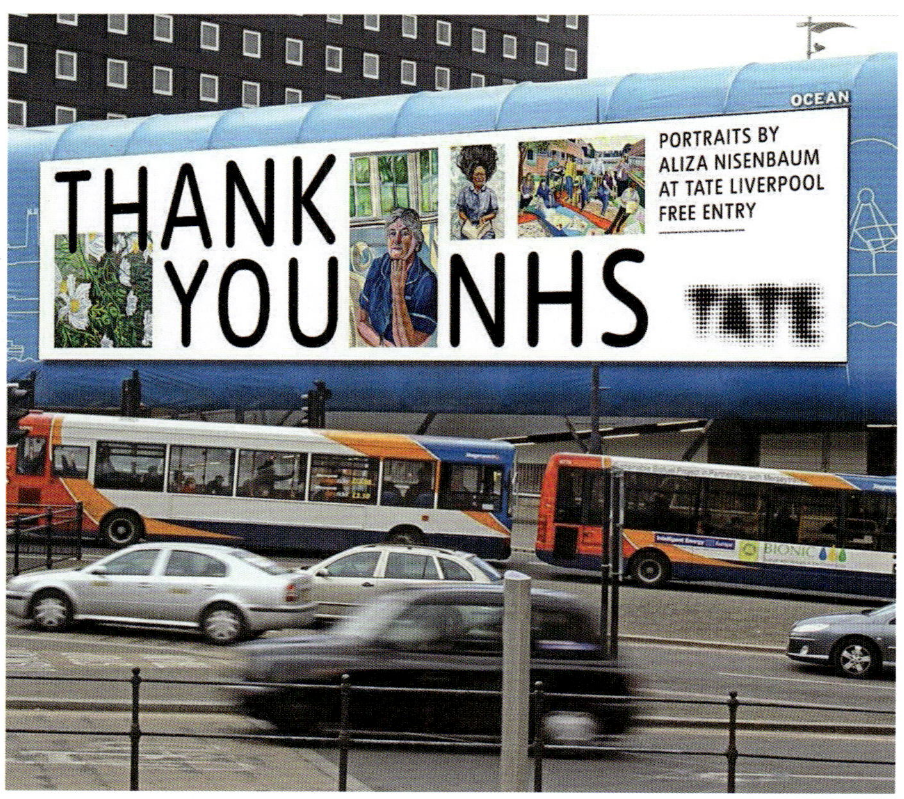

Messages of thanks to the NHS featured on outdoor billboards across
Liverpool during the opening weekend of the exhibition in December 2020

to show a window into them. The most fun part of the work was collaborating with the individuals, because again it takes me out of my preconceived notions of how an image should be. Stephen set up a home studio for a yoga practice with his husband where they give online lessons and take a break from their demanding jobs. We decided to portray him in a restful pose with his sleeve rolled up to show his intricate tattoo, in front of his peacock curtains and houseplants and with his dog Archie. Ryan, who became a father during this time, was tending to his allotment, so I painted him outside holding his son who was wearing a striking sunflower onesie. Shari was photographed by the river, and I painted her in this peaceful setting which is so far removed from the hectic environment of the intensive care unit that she described when we spoke. Emily was also going out into nature when she could, after her very gruelling shifts as a critical care nurse. She said her hobby was rock-climbing, an activity she compared to the intensity of nursing.

The notion of care is very prominent in this project – not only the care that your sitters provide for their patients, but also the way they care for each other and self-care, which has become very important during this time. The paintings of flowers that you made are not just a symbolic way of giving thanks to your sitters, but they also reflect your own self-care. You encountered these flowers during your daily walks in lockdown in LA, which many people did to reconnect with nature and for our mental health. Could you speak about how those different forms of care manifested themselves while you were creating these portraits?

Since we all had to sit back and stay home, we re-evaluated how we were going at a million miles per hour before the pandemic – ignoring the limits of our bodies. I found nature to be a place of profound renewal for myself and of strength as I went into this project. I was watching the subjects I was painting, but also my work made me more self-aware, and I would reflect on this experience during my walks. That's why I decided to draw the flowers and plants I'd encounter on my long walks in LA and include them in the exhibition. This was my way of sending a painted gesture of care in the form of a bouquet for the hard work they were doing.

The Alder Hey group paintings are a reflection on a particular initiative of care by the hospital staff. Lalith was one of my first collaborators, helping me brainstorm on what shape the composition would take. He encouraged his whole A&E (accident and emergency) team to apply to our open call and be depicted as a group. 'Team Time' is a storytelling initiative at the hospital where each person would listen to their colleague's experience during the pandemic. Each one made a drawing of this experience, and I re-transcribed these in the paintings.

This type of care was also present at the other hospitals; Jackie's work as a chaplain involved being there to support the exhausted staff from the hospital, to provide relief from the stress and fear that they all faced.

Many of us offered informal care and mutual aid to each other during the pandemic – not only professional care workers in hospitals, but the countless number of parents and families dedicated to this kind of labour. For example, Claire spoke about the struggle of balancing her work with childcare and

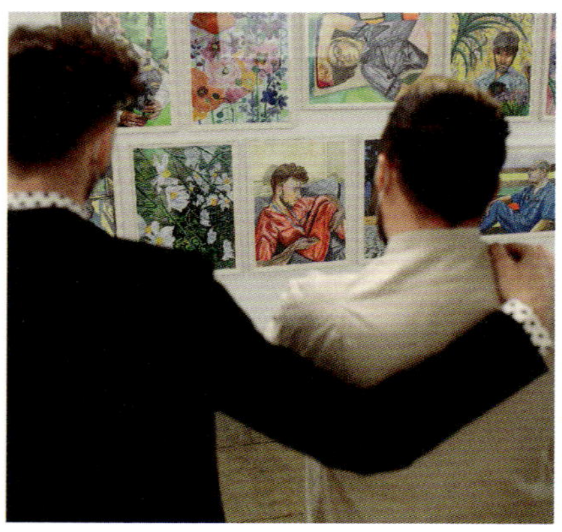

Alan and his partner view his portrait at Tate Liverpool

homeschooling, while Sue was doing the shopping for her brother, who had to shield due to an autoimmune disease. The attention on informal care work feels more prominent now. It's very gendered; in the news, they keep talking about how women particularly have been affected, because so much of their work was unpaid labour. And if we really take a moment to reflect on what our newfound appreciation for care work implies, it should transform our very notions of ourselves towards ones that are less independent. The vulnerability we have all felt during the pandemic underscores the fundamental responsibility we all have towards each other.

As part of this new commission, you wanted to honour those people who have worked endlessly and selflessly during the Covid-19 pandemic. It was very important to portray not only the faces but also the voices of all those in the NHS that contribute to that collective effort. In general, I think, you see your work as a collaboration between yourself and the subjects of your paintings. You're led by a dialogue between you and your sitter, and there's a level of vulnerability on both sides. Could you elaborate on how the portraits evolve in this way?

Naveena is a good example of this selflessness. She was training as a nurse because she wanted to help people, and what better way to start than during the pandemic? She was afraid of bringing the virus home and her loved ones getting ill, but practically her whole family opted in to work on the front lines. I depicted her reading a book, taking a break, yet alertly looking directly at the viewer. Perhaps showing her at rest was a way to reflect the various ways healthcare workers were put in such vulnerable situations. Colin also decided to opt in as part of the 'Stand Up, Step Forward, Save Lives' initiative. I wanted to include people in a variety of roles in my works as a way of representing those whose labour is essential but is often unrecognised. For example, Sue's work as a housekeeper at Alder Hey might not be immediately visible to others, but she had the responsibility of making sure her colleagues had the correct PPE (personal protective equipment) to minimise exposure, and her role was a very important one, as well as a stressful one for her and her family. Kevin is dedicated to his role as a porter and has a great understanding of how daunting it can be for a child to come into hospital. The kindness he shows his patients as he moves them between wards and his poignant stories about loss were incredibly moving.

Not only did each person contribute their story – I was also sharing with them my experience being in LA during the pandemic, away from my home in New York City. The collaborative effort was also felt at the opening of the exhibition at Tate, when the subjects of the works got to meet each other. I've seen this in other projects I've worked on as well – the act of painting a group can make new connections possible, bringing people together that might not have come in contact otherwise. Calum, for example, realised that some of the samples he had been using for his research had been taken by Colin. Jessica and Alan had been taught at Edge Hill University by Calum's wife, so they had a reunion at the opening. Sadly, because of the restrictions, I couldn't travel for the opening, but I learned that staff at the gallery itself, such as members of the front of house teams, stopped by to personally thank the sitters for the work they have done over the past year. And the gallery staff also opened the exhibition privately for Ryan, who was delayed and missed the opening.

This project had multiple positive outcomes that really breached the gap between art and life. The sitters knew that my gallery and I were intending to make donations to the NHS from the proceeds of each sale of the works when they eventually are sold, and they asked for these funds to be allocated to staff wellbeing, which we will do. The hospitals were grateful to hear this. All of a sudden, the NHS were talking about the works and highlighting the healthcare workers from their staff that I had depicted. I hope I can do more of that, to represent those who might not otherwise have entered into a gallery and to finally include their voices.

It was such a beautiful moment to have all the sitters in the gallery seeing their portraits and also being able to meet each other. It's been such a special project, and you've given us at Tate the opportunity to say thank you to these people, not just the sitters but everyone that they represent – people working for the NHS, but also all key workers who have put themselves on the front line in order to help others.

Thank you, Tamar! And like Kevin said, when Covid restrictions loosen, and I can make it over to Liverpool, he's going to take me out to a pub for a proper Scouse stew, so hopefully we'll get to celebrate in person, all of us together!

The following texts are from the sitters, reflecting on their experiences in conversations with Aliza Nisenbaum in the summer of 2020.

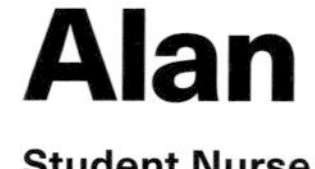

Alan

Student Nurse

I was close to finishing my nursing degree when Covid first hit. Initially the university closed, but healthcare students could apply for NHS placements to help with the pandemic while completing our qualifications. After six weeks of waiting, I got the call to confirm my placement. I was so happy, as it was the last thing I needed to complete in order to qualify as a nurse!

At the time, my mother was seriously ill in hospital. The day before I was due to start my placement, my sister phoned me to say that my mum's ventilator settings were being lowered, which I knew wasn't good. My dad and I went straight to the hospital, where we met my two sisters. The nurse looking after my mum explained what was happening. I held my mum's hand as I looked at her monitors and I could see her heart rate become erratic, then I noticed that there was a long pause on her ventilator and I knew that she had passed away. The feeling was one of true loss, a different kind of pain that I'd never felt in my life.

I still went to my placement induction the next day, as I knew my mum would have wanted me to, and I wanted to make her proud. She raised me to never give up, and whenever I had setbacks she was always there to pick me up and give me the strength to carry on. When I woke up on the first morning of my placement I noticed her hairbrush and I put some of her hair in a locket so that I could always keep part of her close to me. I've since finished my qualifications and I work as a nurse at the Walton Centre.

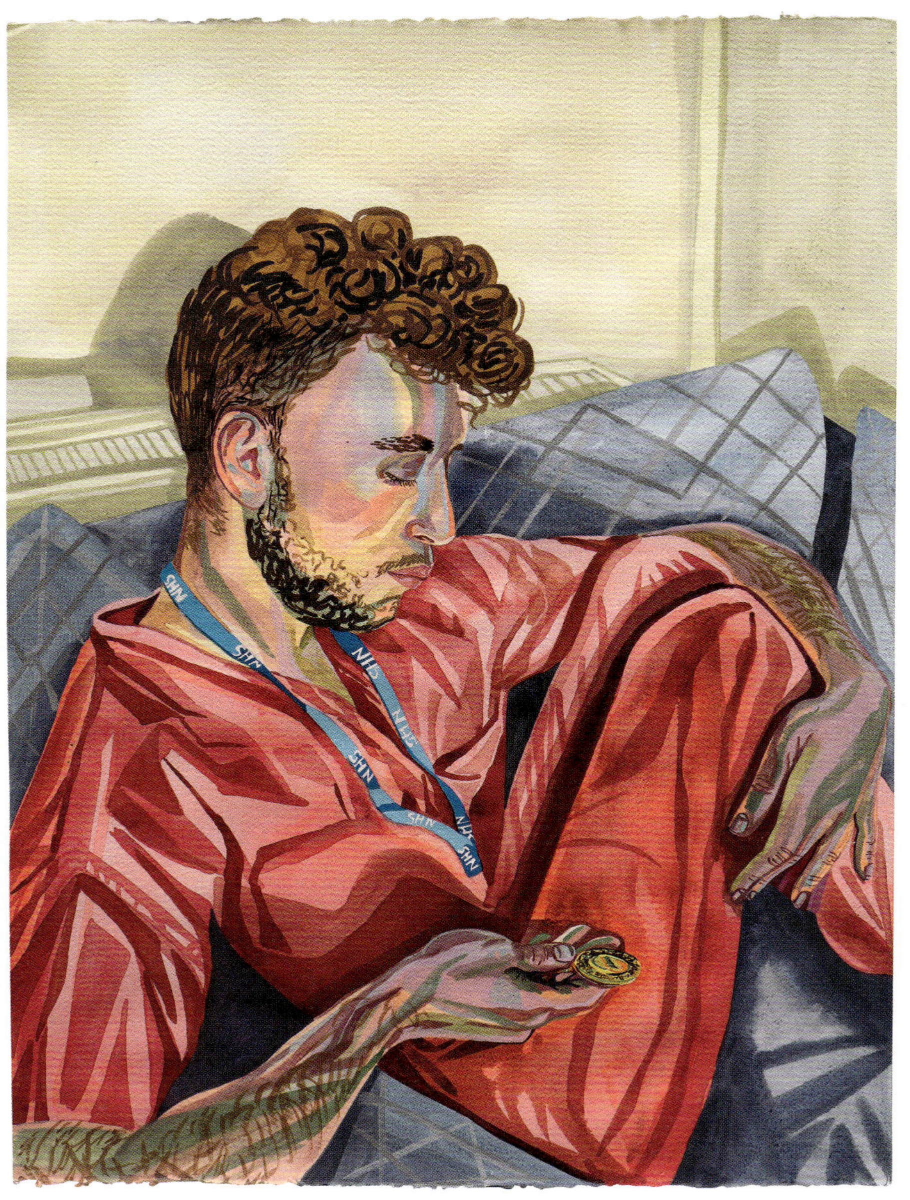

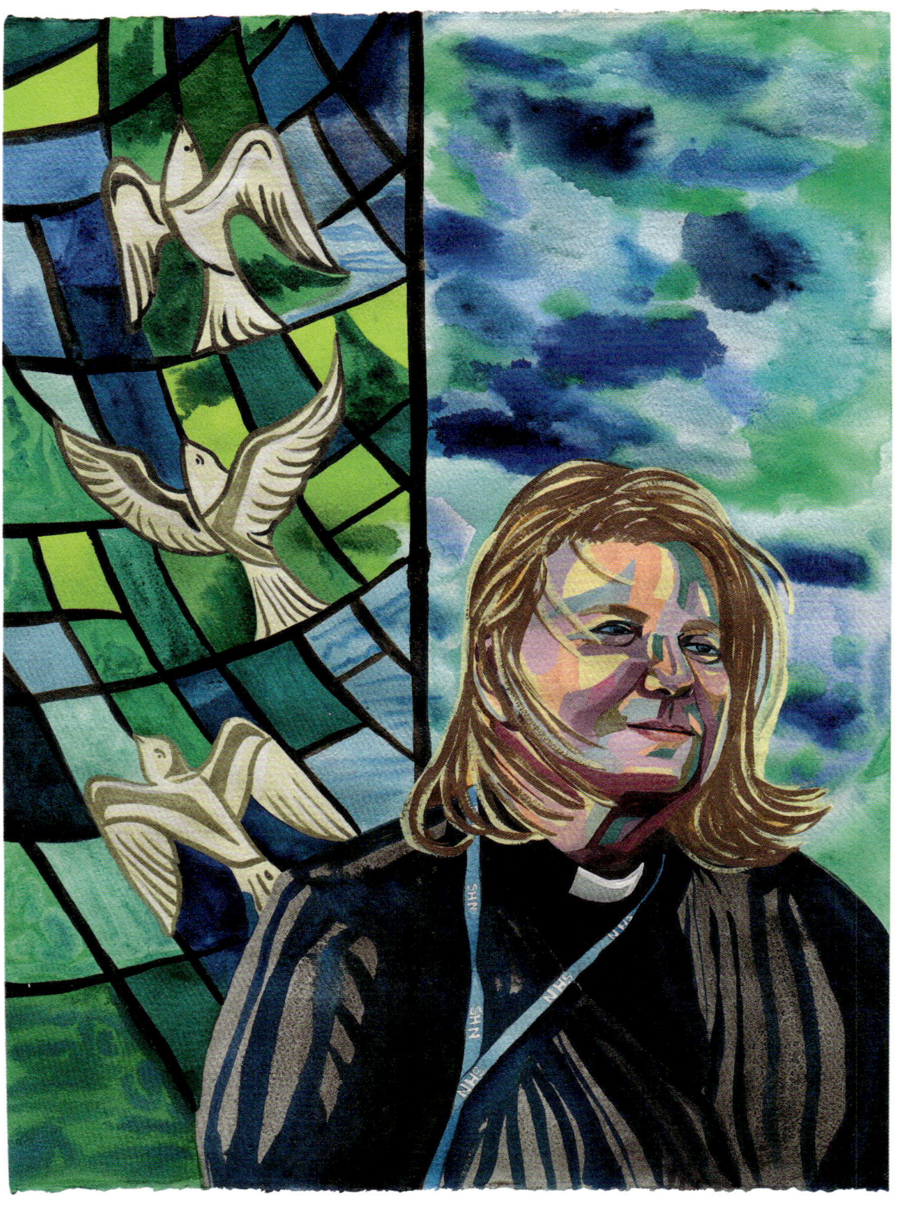

Reverend Jackie

Hospital Chaplain

The job of a chaplain is all about support – whether it's listening to somebody or allowing people the freedom to cry, scream or shout. During the pandemic it has been very difficult because often we couldn't physically go to see patients and their relatives. It wasn't necessarily only people of faith – it's everybody – although I've found a lot of people have come to faith during this, especially when they'd lost somebody. It brought comfort, to feel that their loved one was resting in heaven and not in any pain. Some people lost quite a few loved ones, that was heart-breaking. Patients in the past have asked me for a hug and I'm a hugger, but now physical contact is not allowed which is very difficult. You couldn't even hold someone's hand.

The people I saw were mostly staff who needed a tremendous amount of support as well. A lot of them were separated from their families and they were scared, they were exhausted. For them to have someone there who they could just come and talk to was important. Their life was centred on work all the time, so to be there for them was really quite a privilege.

I was really struck by the care that came out of society during this time. I hope, I really pray, that it will continue afterwards.

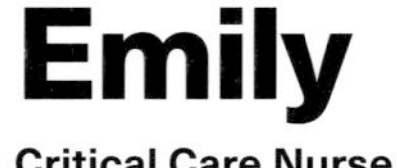

Emily

Critical Care Nurse

I was working as a critical care nurse and then during the Covid pandemic we converted our unit into an intensive care unit. It was challenging because we don't usually look after those types of patients, but we had to. We had ventilator patients on the unit for about two months, which was a very intense time. We did twelve-hour shifts and I ended up on six weeks of night shifts. Nothing resembled normality. Everyone was wearing full PPE; you couldn't recognise anybody. We would wear PPE for four or five hours at a time, without eating or drinking or going to the bathroom because you were aware of not wanting to use extra PPE if you had to take it all off.

Through most of it I was running on adrenaline, it's only now that I've got time to process it. Now there are a lot of us who experience trauma, like flashbacks and emotions that are very close to the surface. Of course it was horrible, but I was glad to be able to be a part of it and do something. I was very proud of our unit and how well everybody adapted, of our team spirit and our camaraderie.

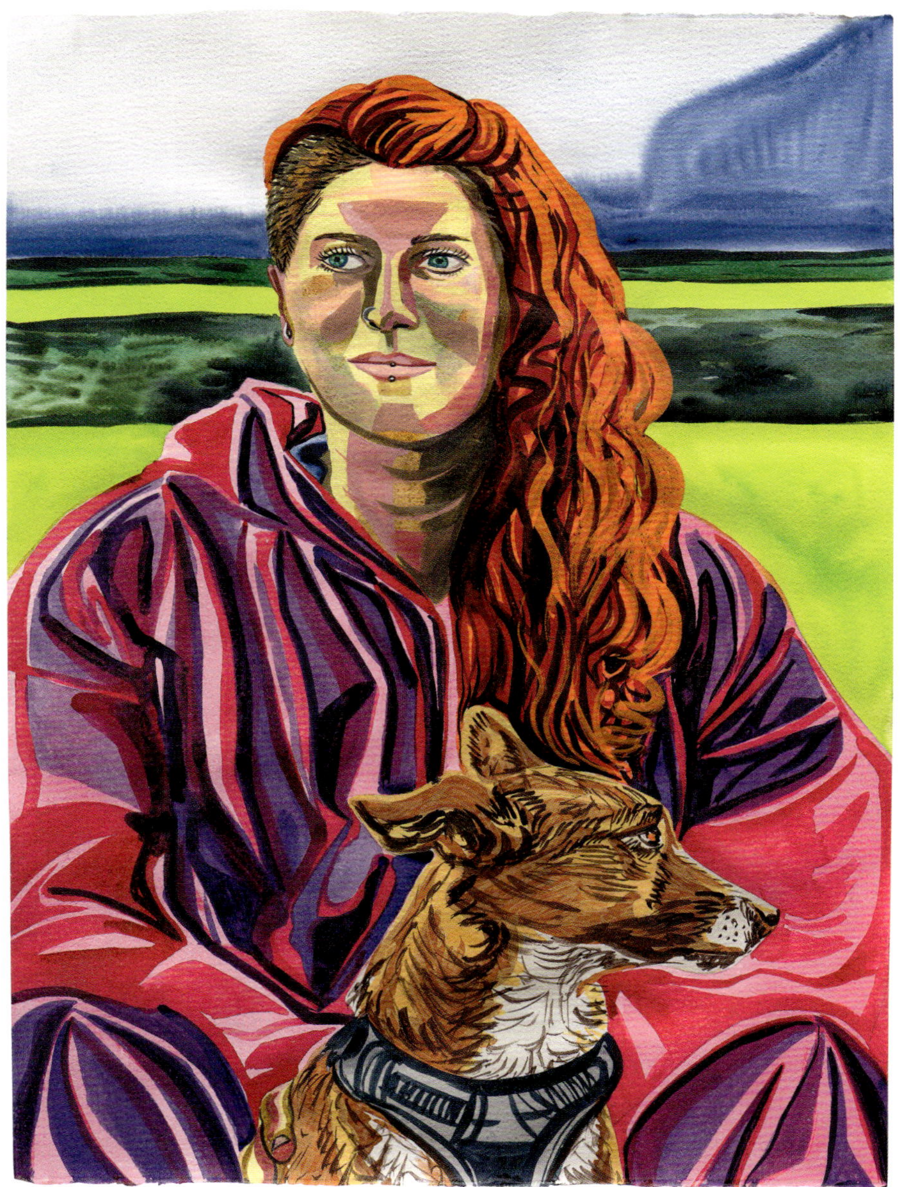

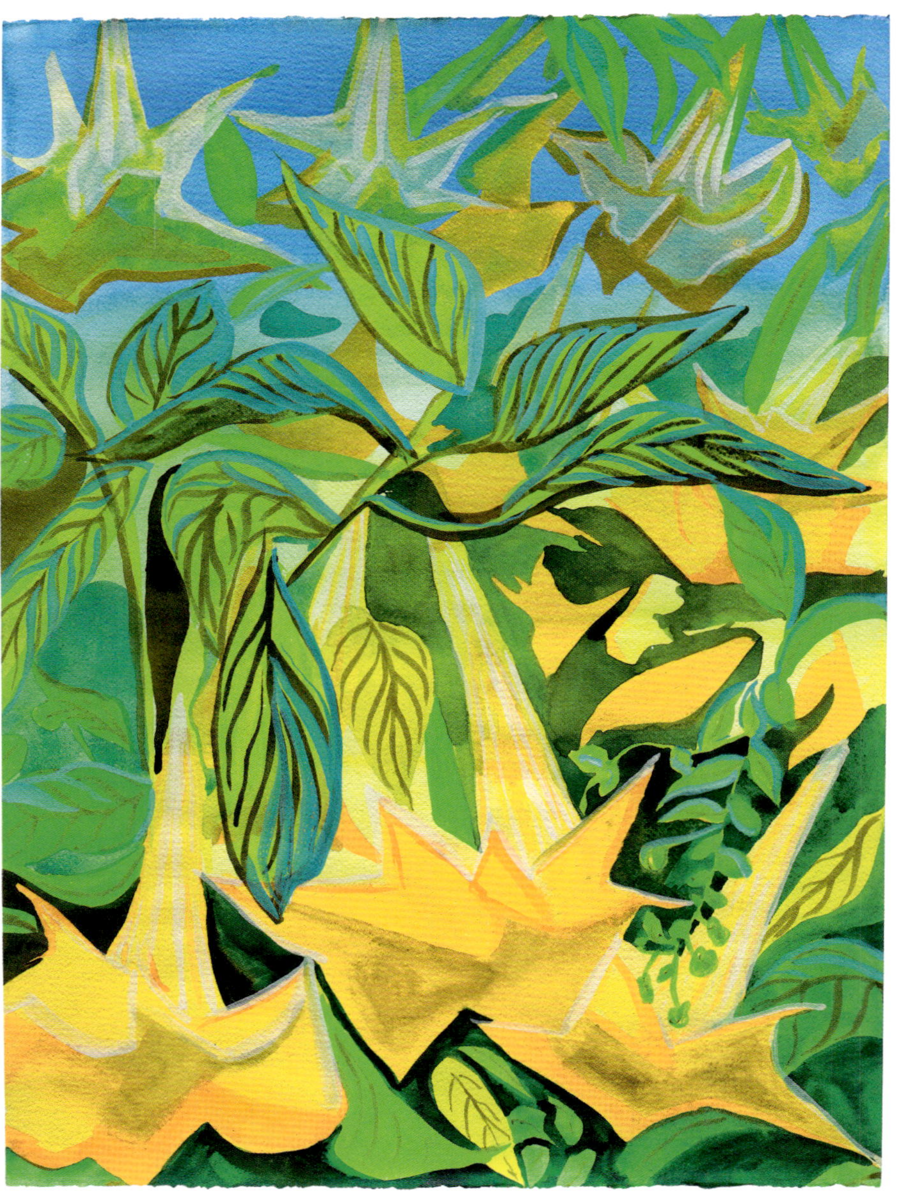

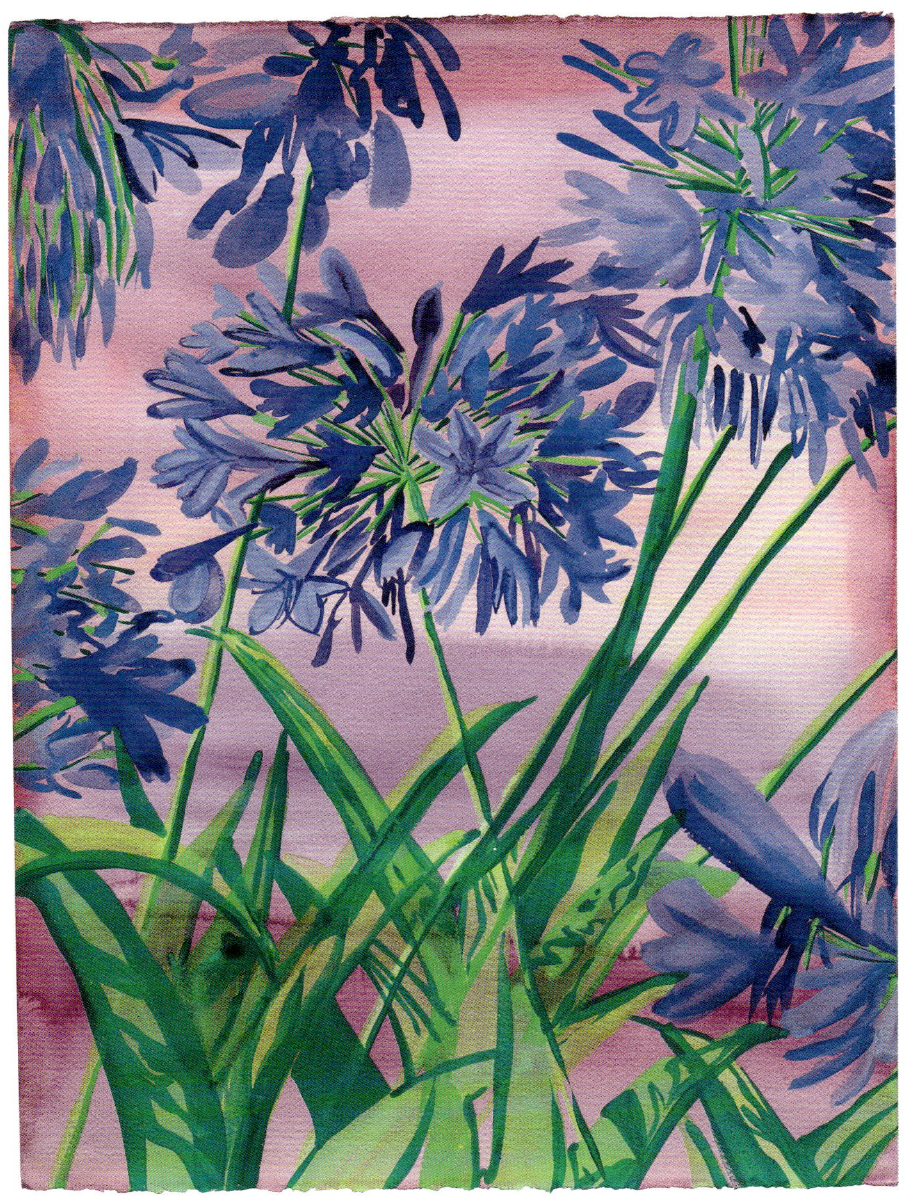

Stephen

Orthoptist

I work as an orthoptist which is an eye specialist in vision and eye movement disorders, and I work with both children and adults. We always try to make the hospital appointments as fun as we can for the children, which is even more important during this confusing and scary time. Though my colleagues and I now have to wear full PPE which can be distressing for kids, the children see it as playing games rather than getting tests. I create a certificate of bravery for each child which I then email to the parents after their appointment. I ask them what their favourite colour is and what their absolute favourite character, cartoon or film is and then create a certificate around this. Some of the parents have told me how much it's meant to the children to get their certificate. Something so small can be so important.

In addition to this job I am a yoga teacher. My husband Paul and I run our own yoga business. This has changed completely since lockdown – we now run our classes online via Zoom. Many have said it's been a lifeline to them but it truly has been to us too. To be able to still connect and keep some normality during this time has been amazing.

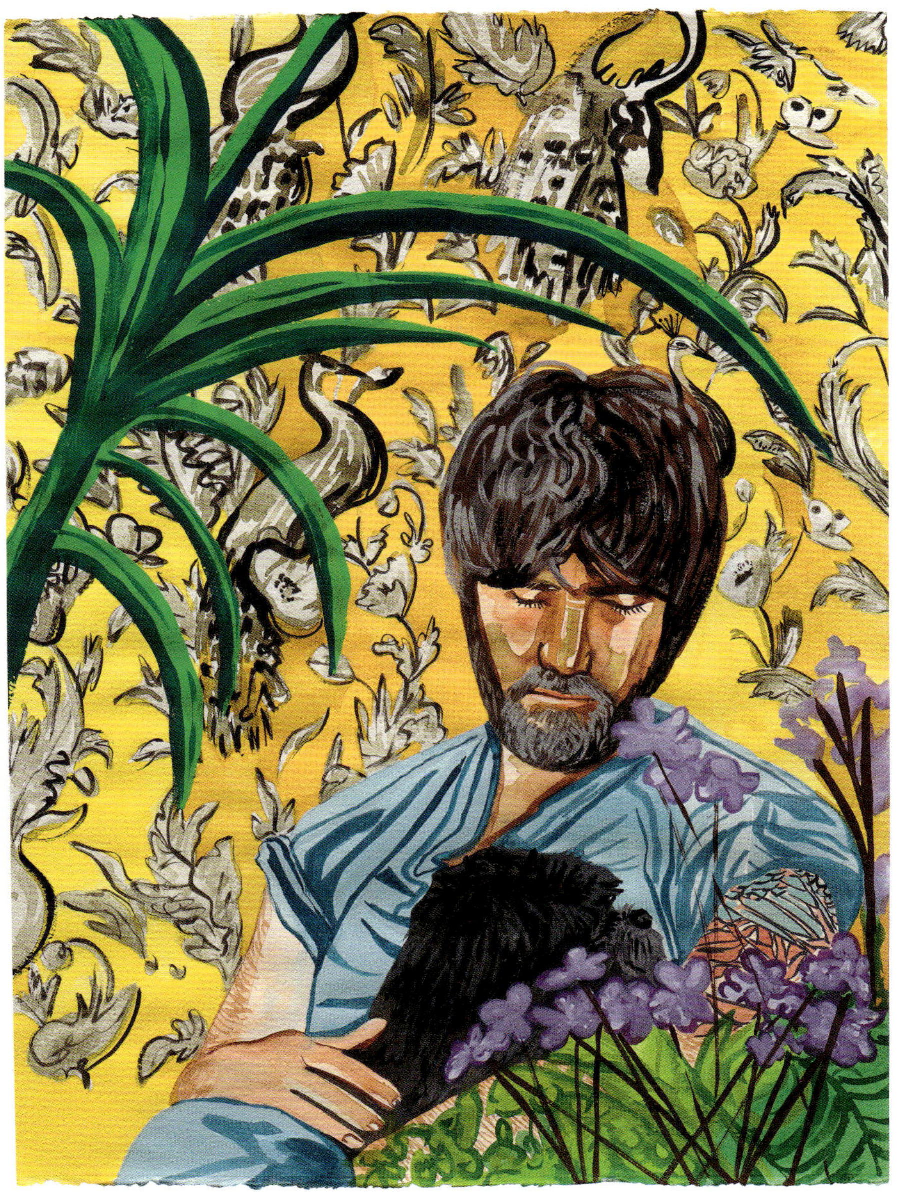

Colin

Nurse and Nursing Lecturer

I was teaching part-time in a university when the
pandemic started. There was a drive from the NHS
with the slogan 'Stand Up, Step Forward, Save Lives' to
encourage medical staff, initially retired people, to
return to work. When this campaign came out I thought
I need to go and do something, I need to be a part of it.

My background is as an ICU (intensive care unit) nurse,
but I have ended up working in all of the general wards
in the hospital. For someone who is used to working
one-on-one, to suddenly be thrown into a situation
where you are treating thirty Covid patients while wearing full PPE was very different. I had to start re-learning
everything and find things out as we went along. Many
NHS staff were redeployed into the acute areas from
other departments and were in a similar situation. I'm
lucky because my academic background is in health
psychology, so I've got an awareness of how to take
care of myself during a time like this. While I haven't felt
the need for any formal intervention or psychological
support, it has been helpful to have great people around
me who are very supportive.

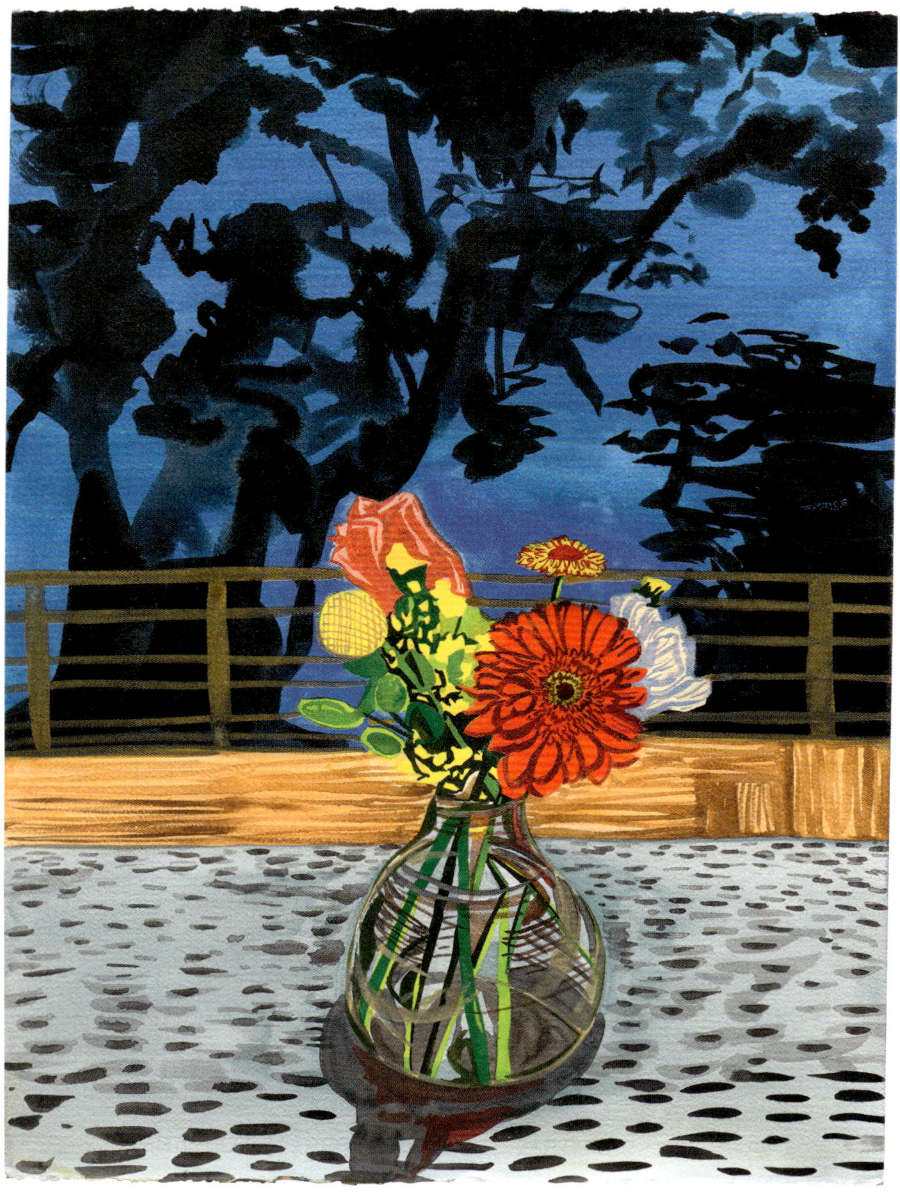

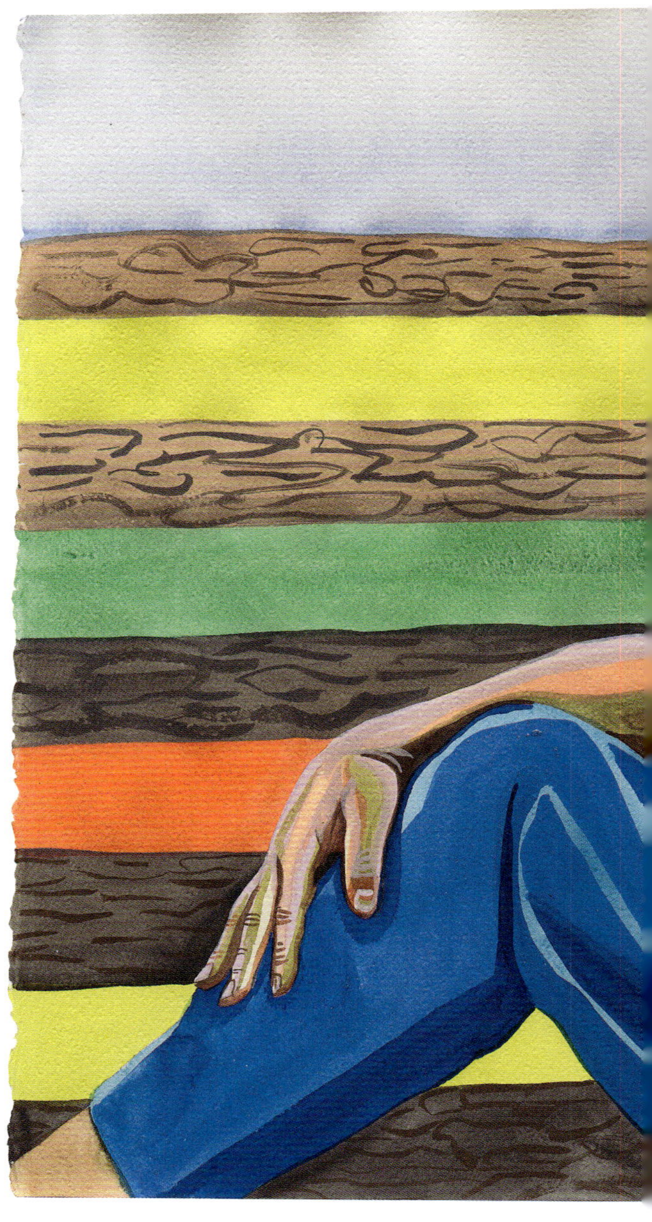

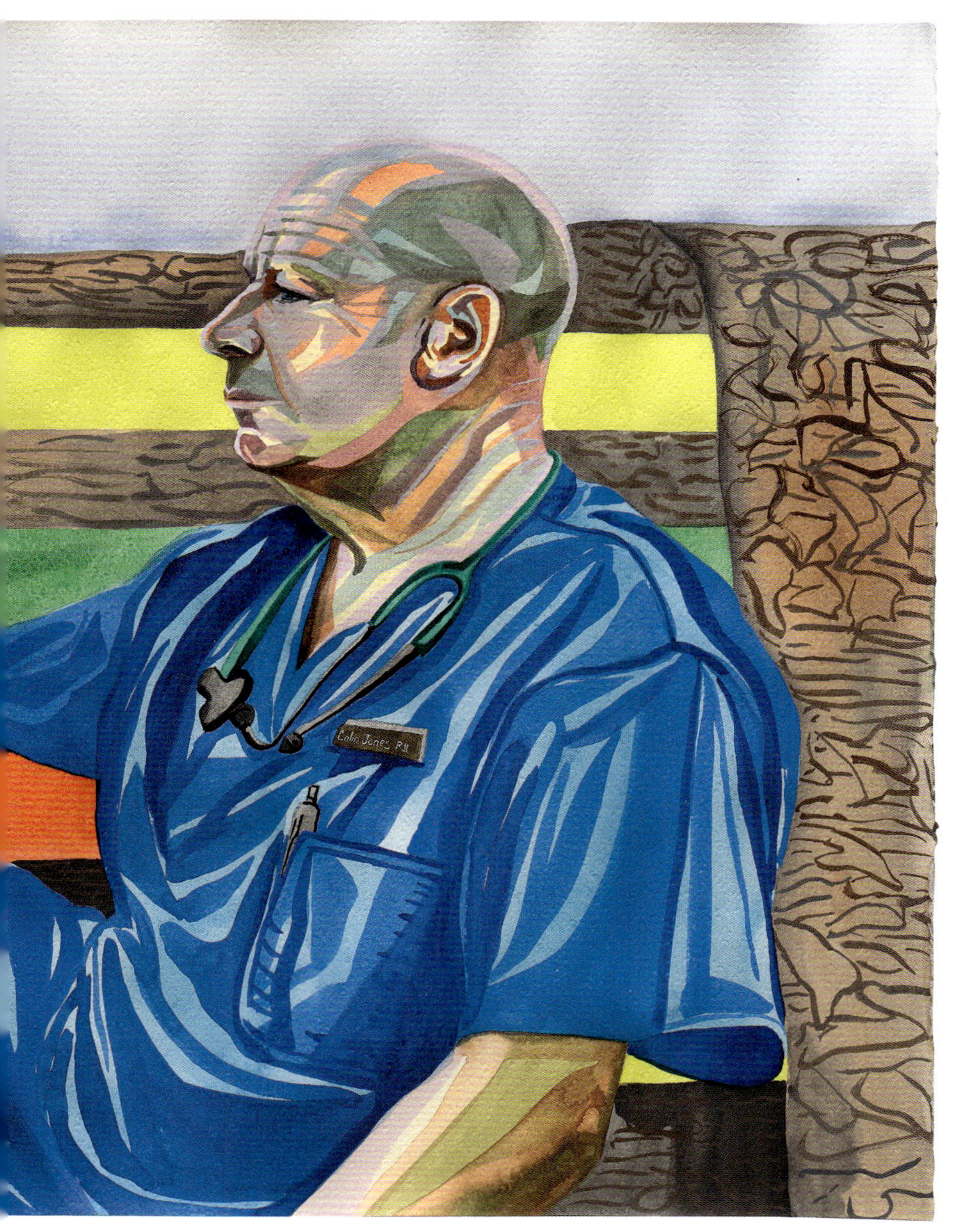

Colin Jones RN

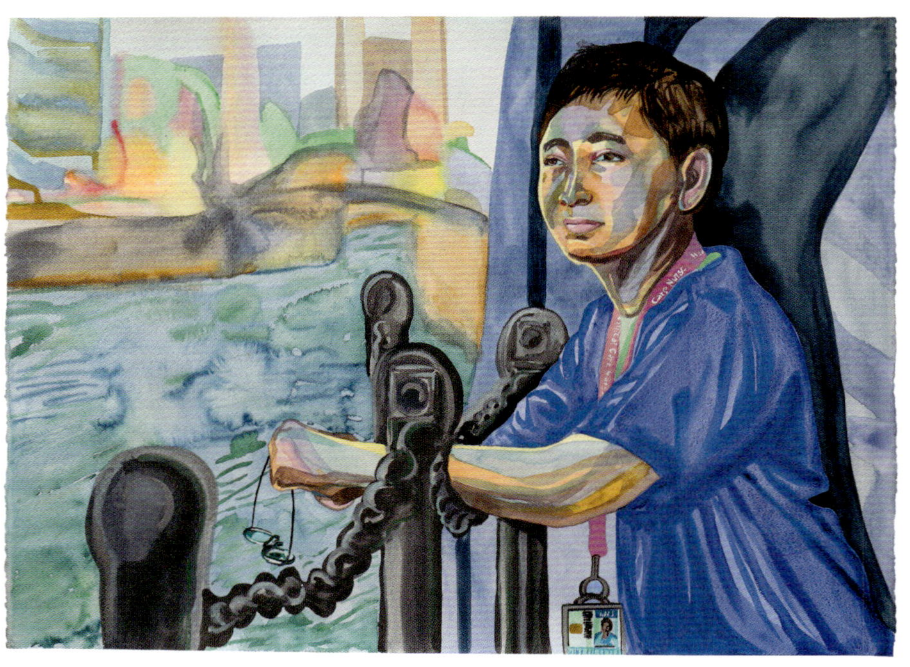

Shari

Intensive Care Nurse

Nobody expected this pandemic. It's brought a lot of bad but we've also seen a lot of good in people. The theatre staff came to help us. Everyone came together during the peak; we had to rely on each other. I imagine it was difficult for them because it's a totally new area and experience, but they just plunged in. We just had to put one foot in front of the other, get through the day and then do it all over again the next day. But we were all like a big family and somehow, we got through it.

It was a very humbling experience but also terrifying because every day you are confronted by your own mortality, as you don't know if you are going to get it, no matter how careful you are. Both my partner and I are from the Philippines. When we went there on holiday earlier this year my partner wasn't able to travel back with me due to the travel ban and our adopted daughter, who still lives in the Philippines, wasn't able to visit. I was here alone during the peak but I was so thankful that they were safe and I didn't have to worry about infecting anyone.

Now that the second wave is here, we're doing it all over again.

Calum

**Professor of Outbreak Medicine
and member of SAGE**

I am one of thousands of people who are part of
the research attempt to beat this virus. In previous
outbreaks, clinical researchers have been deeply
frustrated by our inability to mount a rapid response.
A group of us set up a global organisation called
ISARIC (International Severe Acute Respiratory
and Emerging Infection Consortium) in 2011 which
identified the need to set up hibernating research
studies in readiness for a future outbreak. Previously
it took at least three months to activate a study. For
Covid-19 it took one phone call because of our prepara-
tions. We were able to recruit the very first cases here
and in other countries. For over 70% of people that
were hospitalized with Covid-19, we know their age, sex
and ethnicity, what treatment they needed in hospital
and sadly what happened to them. It's a privilege to
have that information but also a burden because you
see what this horrendous virus is doing to people.
At the start of the outbreak I could see that it was killing
one in three people that came into hospital and many
people were saying it was nothing to worry about.
Now, thanks to research and improved care, we have
reduced deaths by half.

I'm often the person that's bringing bad news to the
public and there are many people that don't want to
hear it. We've got to persuade people that we are
working for their wellbeing and that life will get better.

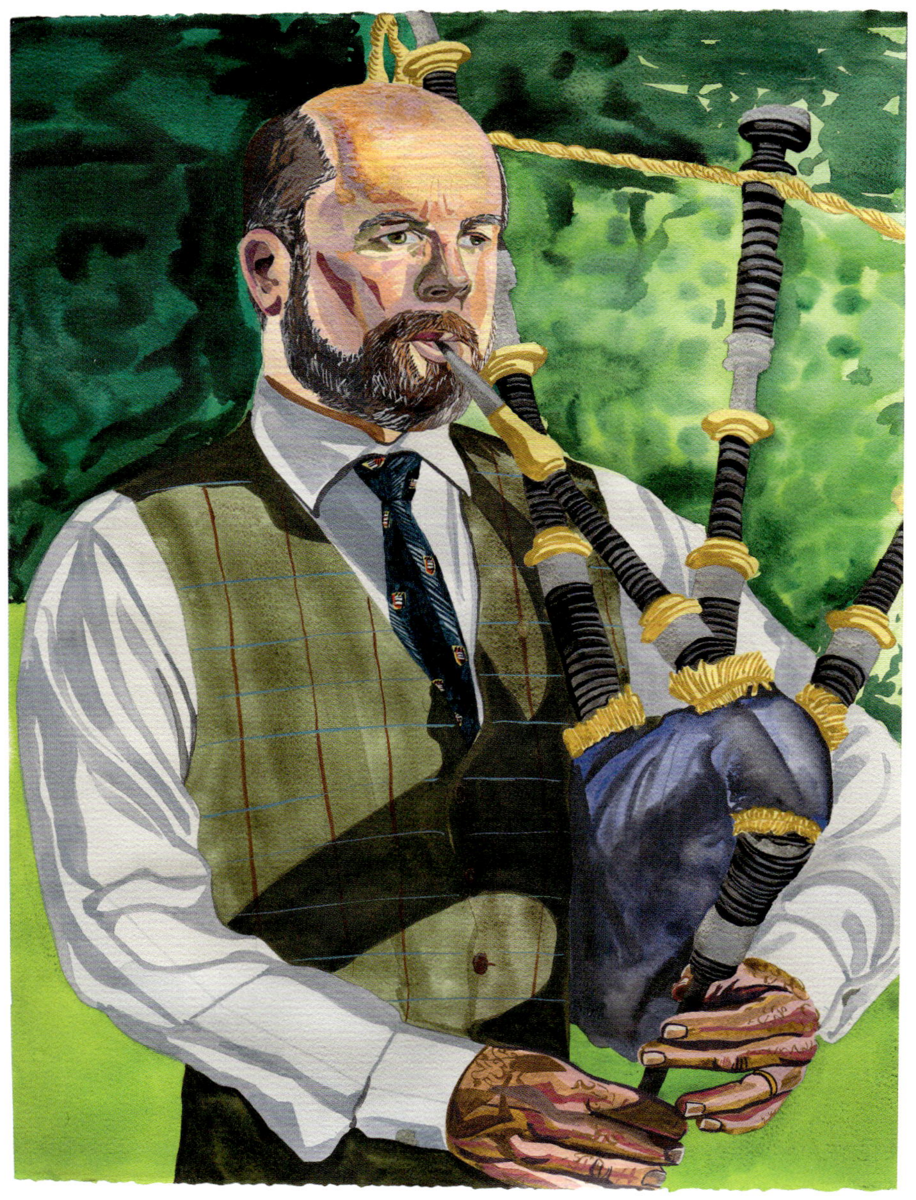

Naveena

Student Nurse

I am a student nurse within mental health and I also am a support worker for people with learning disabilities. My mother is an ICU nurse at Alder Hey; both my sisters are student nurses and several of my aunts also work in healthcare. At the start of the pandemic student nurses were asked if they would work on the front line to help out, and we all decided to volunteer for this. My twin sister worked on a Covid ward and my younger sister worked on a critical care ICU, while I opted to go on a mental health ward. Because I lived in the same house with my mother and younger sister, we were all concerned about bringing the virus back home. My twin sister was working further away and as she was working directly with Covid patients I was very worried about her being directly affected. We had never been apart for that long, so that was incredibly difficult. I was supposed to finish my nursing degree at the end of July and I had planned to go travelling. Unfortunately, due to the pandemic my plans changed quite radically, but hopefully I can travel when this is all over.

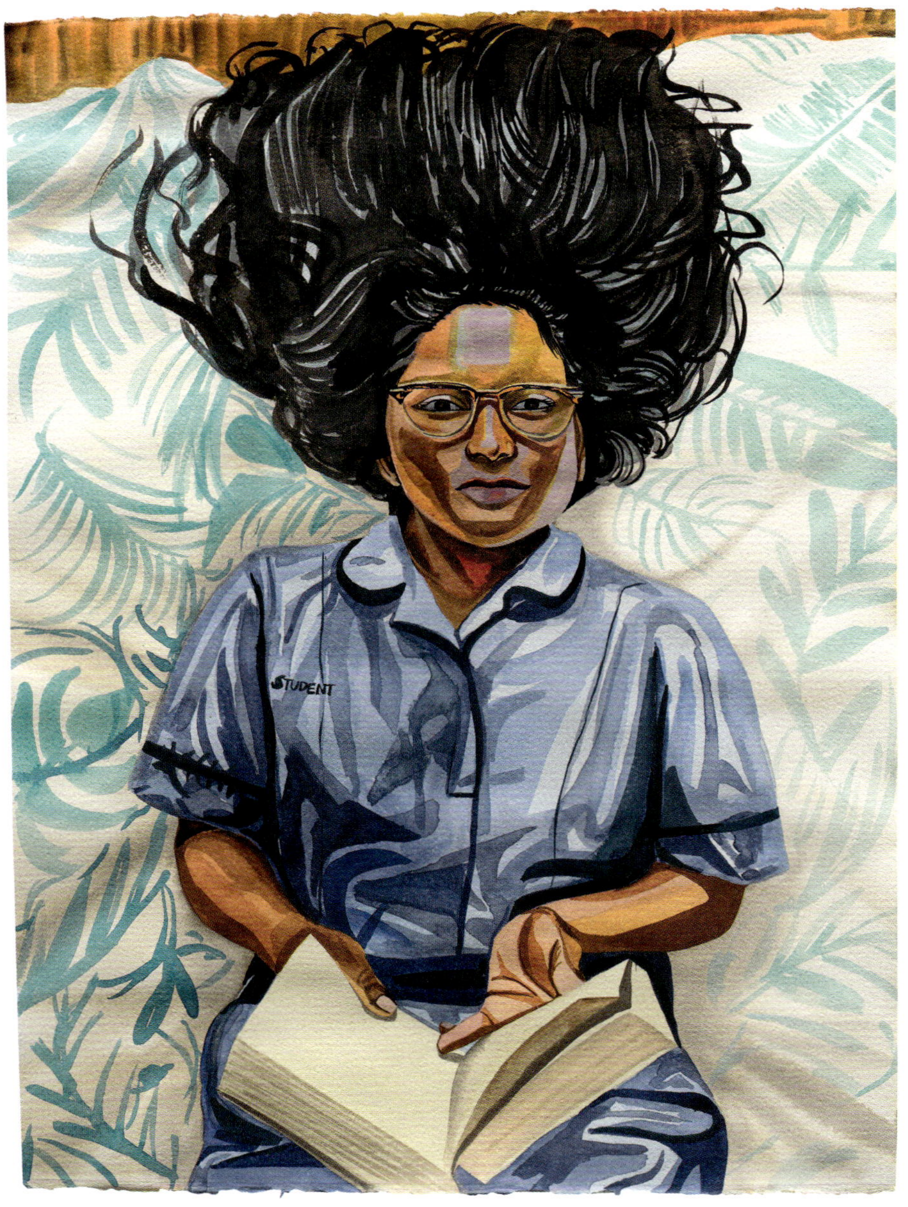
STUDENT

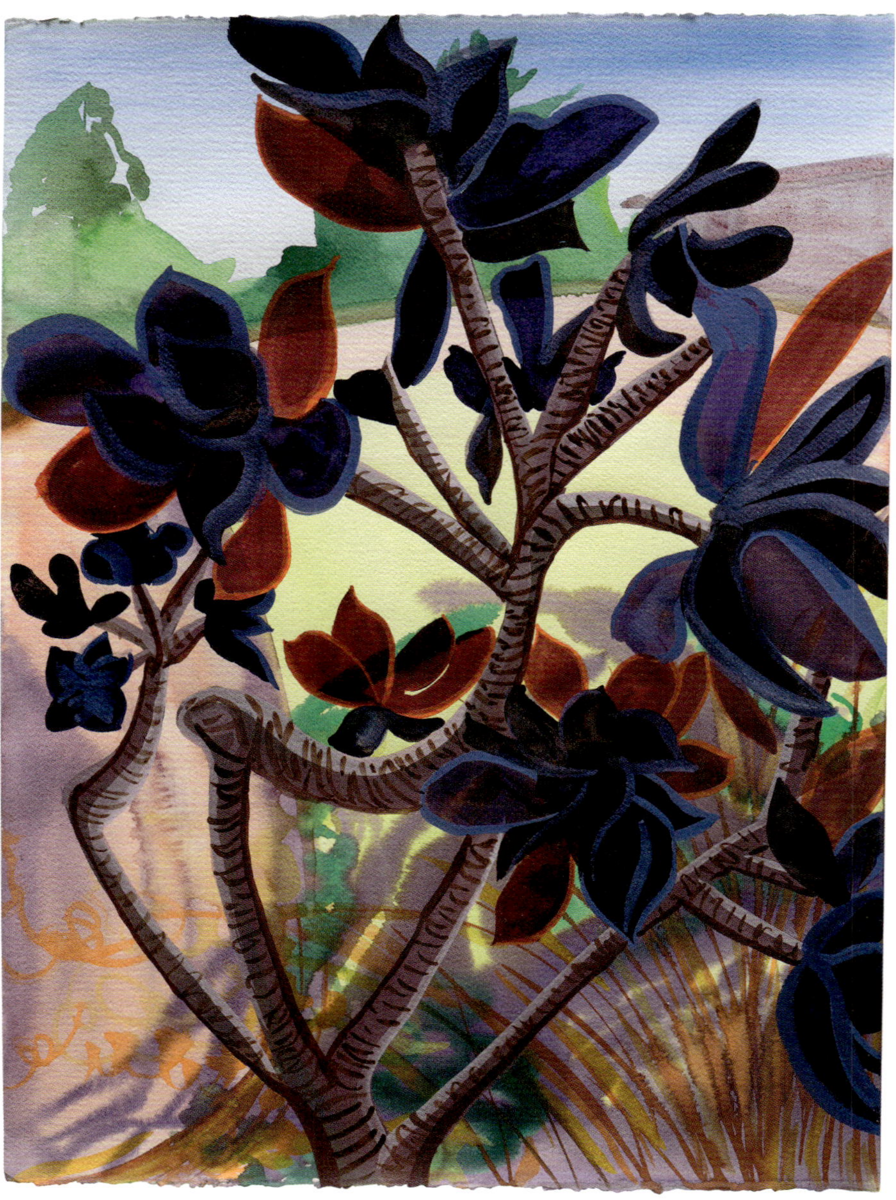

Jessica

Student Nurse

I'm training to be a nurse and I was on placement in
a hospital at the start of the pandemic. As there is
a huge shortage of nurses I decided to keep working
and it was a proper learning experience. The clapping
for the NHS on Thursday evenings was amazing.
I loved it, but there is not enough government support
for staff working on the ground. It was hard to hear
that nurses would not be given a pay rise, because as
nice as the clapping was, it won't pay the bills.

My Nan is my inspiration. In the 1950s she married
a Nigerian man while living in a very white, industrial
mining town, so I salute her for her bravery. They
had three children, including twins, but he left her so
she had to raise them by herself. Like me, she went
back to college to study nursing at a slightly older age,
while taking life drawing classes in the evenings. She
inspired me to become a nurse, and she, along with my
eldest daughter who is a budding artist herself, is the
reason I wanted to take part in this project.

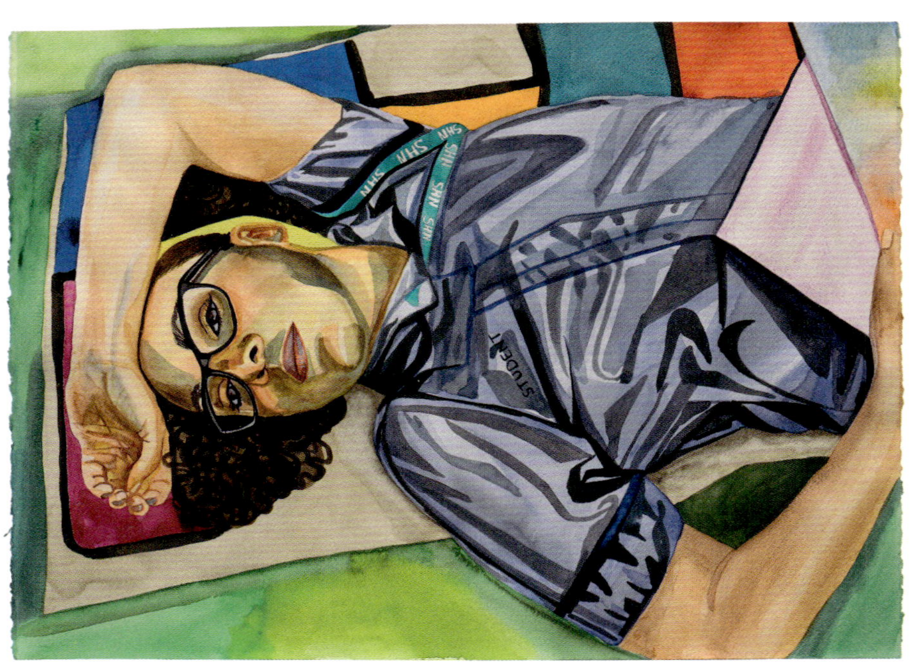

SHU
STUDENT

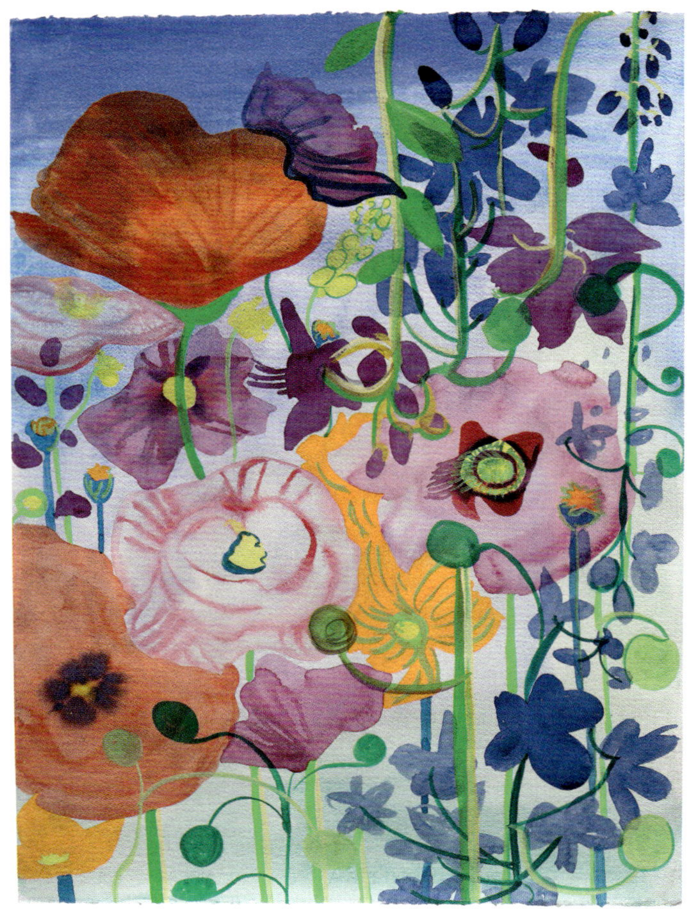

Ryan

Respiratory Doctor in Training

I'm a junior doctor training in respiratory medicine, currently doing research, which I've been doing for a couple of years up until March, when everything changed. The research I'd been working on was halted and I was called in to help out. So pretty much the next day, I was back on the wards. It was stressful because at the time the tests we had took about four days for the results to come back, so you had to be really careful and assume that everybody had it. I remember our first patient who tested positive. I frantically thought, 'What interaction have I had with them? How much risk have I put myself at?'

Our son was born in mid-May. In March, when the outbreak really began, my wife was around twenty-six weeks pregnant, so she was isolating at home. I was going to work, so I had to be extra careful. As soon as I got home I would take off all my clothes, run upstairs and shower, making sure I didn't touch anything.

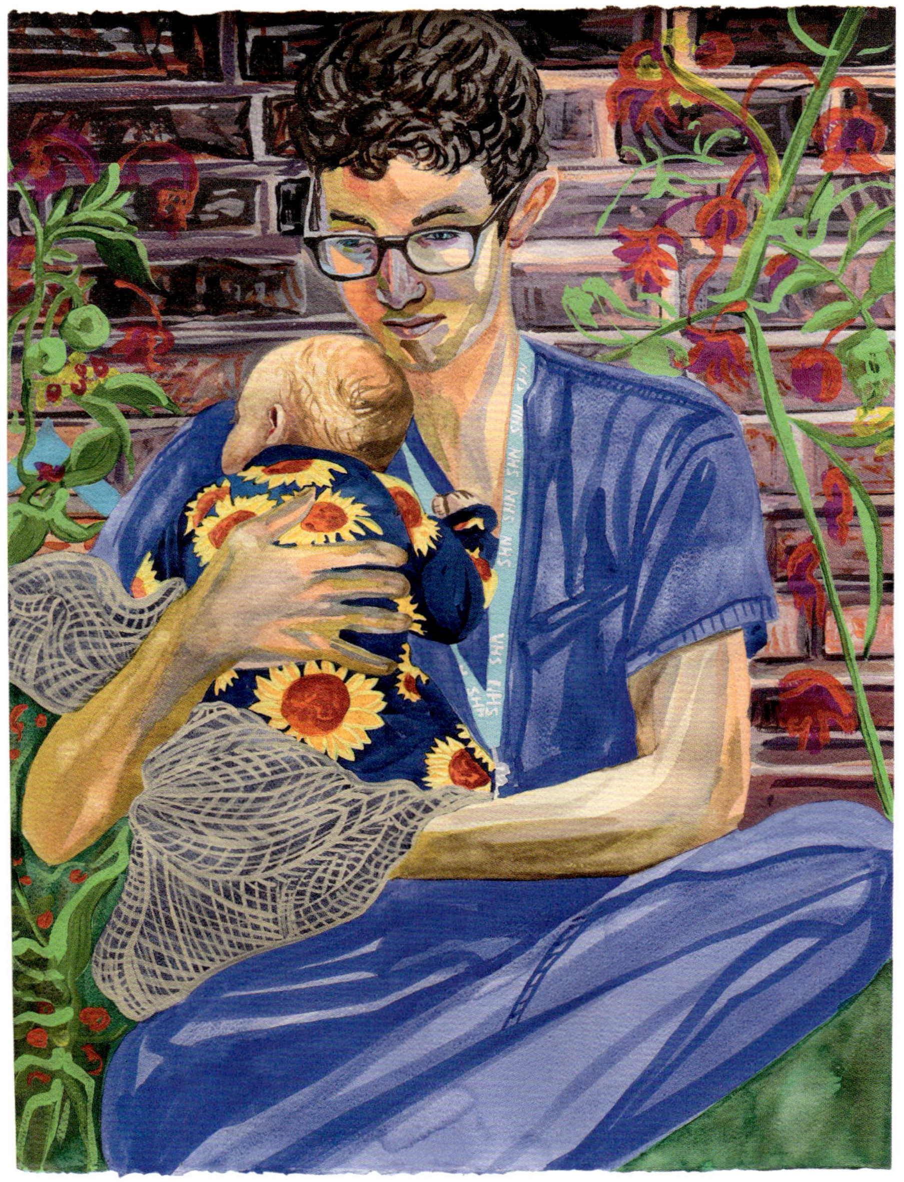

Ann

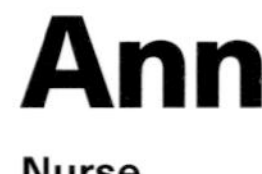

Nurse

I've been a nurse for a lot of years. It sounds a bit
cheesy, but I've never wanted to be anything else.
I count myself as being incredibly lucky, because I get
excited about going to work every morning. I'm just
coming into my thirty-fifth year working in addiction.
With some of these patients, I know their families, they
allow me to join in with their triumphs, commiserate
with their sorrows, and it's such a privilege.

During the outbreak, the nurses I manage were
redeployed to the wards to do general nursing, and
only myself and my deputy have stayed. We usually do
lots of health promotion but many of our clients haven't
been allowed into the hospital, so we've only been
dealing with people who are really sick.

Coronavirus has brought everyone together – people
are going the extra mile, disputes are put aside. I've
seen great acts of kindness, not only to patients, but
also to each other. I've been really touched by this.

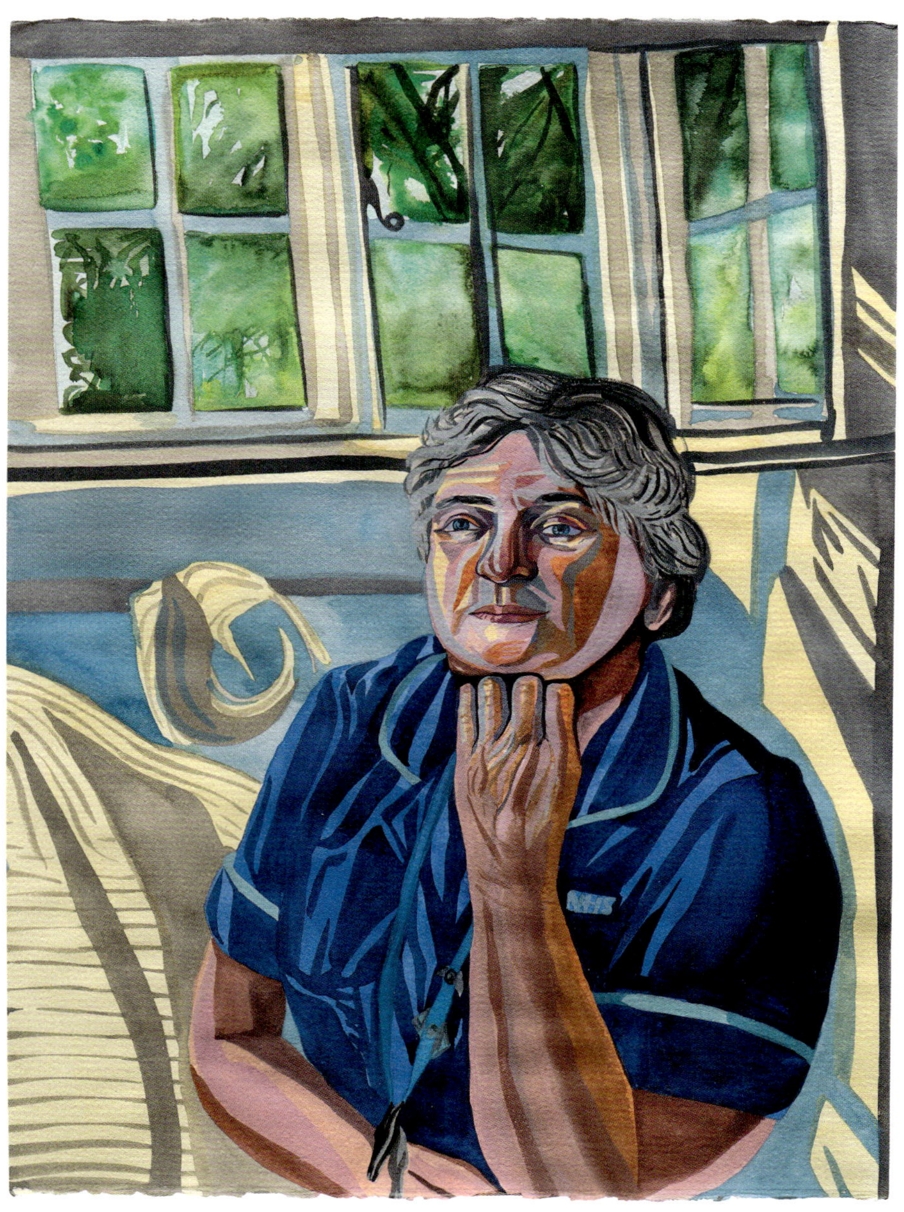

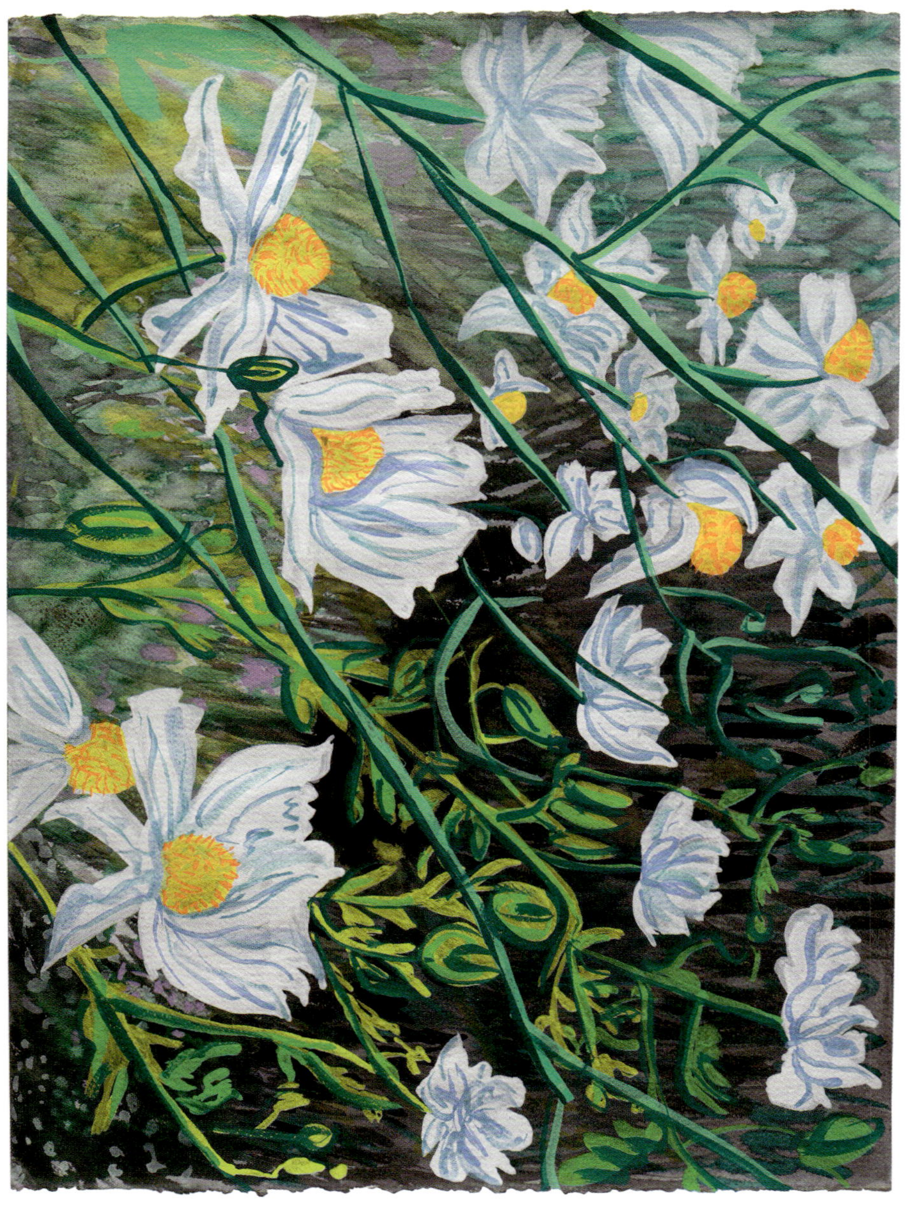

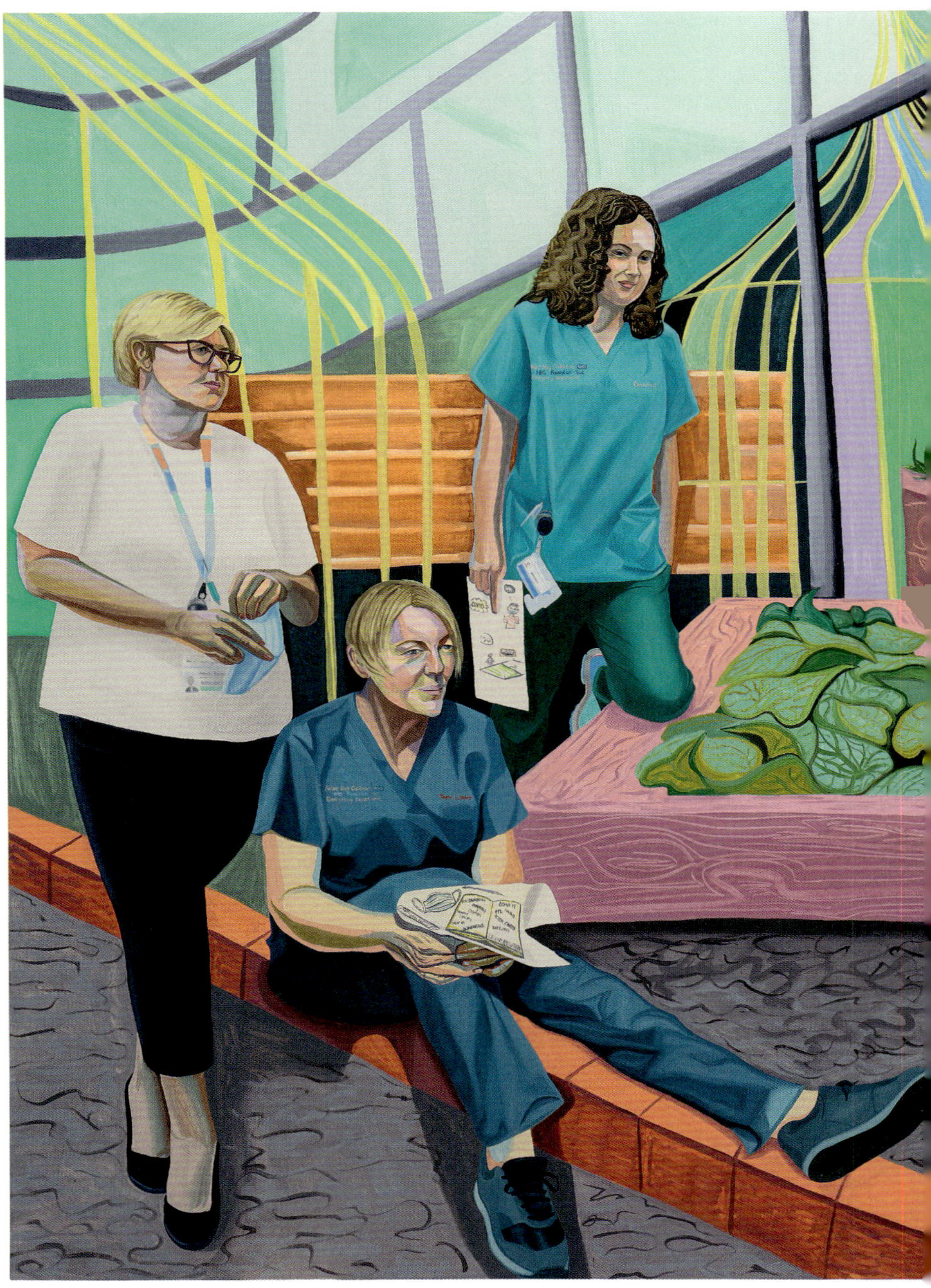

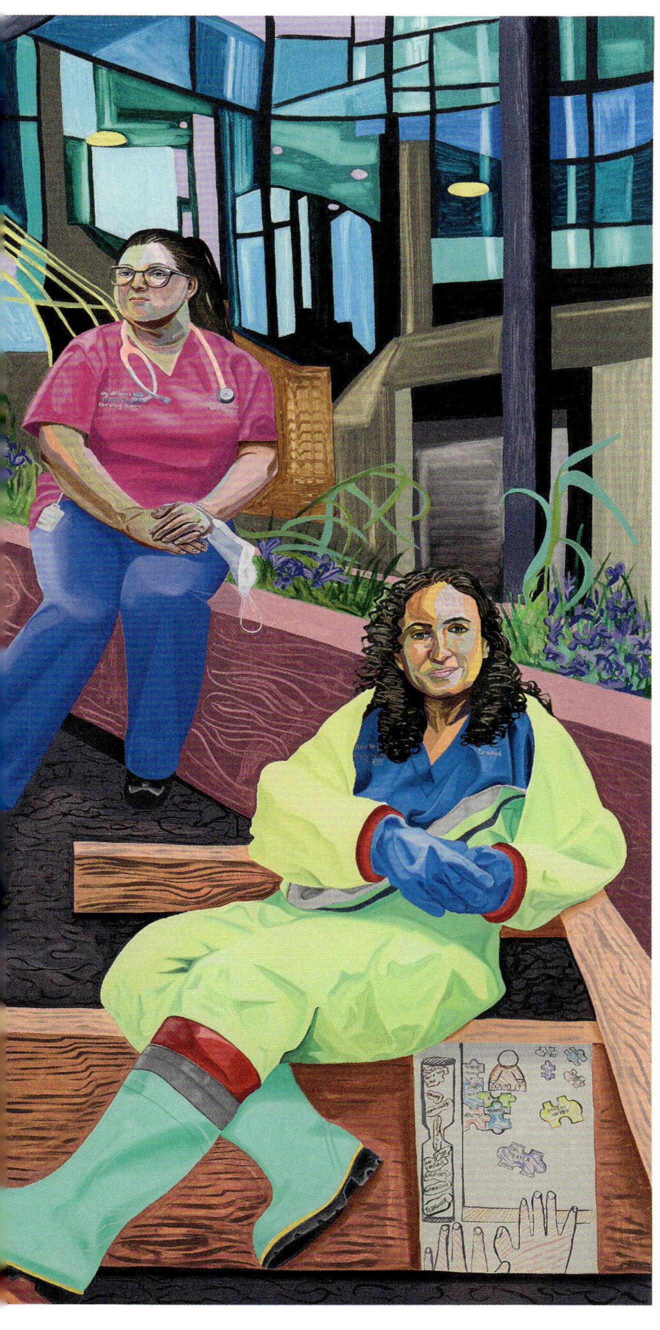

Amanda

Head of Acute Care

I have been qualified for over thirty years and spent twenty-seven of those within an acute paediatric setting. My current role is Head of Acute Care – essentially this is the lead nurse for the emergency department and assessment unit, general paediatric ward, diabetes team and the acute care team. This means that I no longer work clinically but I really enjoy people management in terms of support and staff development, particularly when you then watch those staff progress in their career or achieve their personal goals.

Covid has changed the way we all work. Every area has been affected by social distancing, PPE changes and requirements or changing staffing levels. At the onset, getting the balance right was difficult as there were daily updates regarding processes, training all the staff and ensuring communications got to everyone. I felt like I was constantly at a planning event. I also couldn't work as closely to support our staff and at times that felt very isolating. I'm now on my own in my office, which can be great for getting work done, but it's also lonely as most of my interaction with others is via the computer screen.

This has been a challenging time for the NHS and something I've never really experienced in my career. I feel that the teams have really stepped up to the mark in dealing with everything expected of them, especially with all the constant changes.

Tracey

Paediatric Nurse Team Leader, Emergency Department

I've worked as a nurse at Alder Hey for twenty years. I'm part of the infection control team and I got involved with Covid quite early, around January when it first started in China. My role was to train all the staff in the correct use of PPE. We've got around sixty of us in the nursing team, plus all the doctors, so it was quite a big task. I had to deliver something like 300 training sessions, which was quite daunting at first!

Back in summer last year I went to be trained at the infectious diseases unit at the adult hospital and it was really helpful that I'd done that training before the Covid outbreak. I was the only one in my department who'd done this, so I felt it was my responsibility to get all my colleagues trained. I ended up making myself sick as I'd worked so many hours and burned myself out. My colleagues were all very supportive and if I had a problem, someone was always available for a chat.

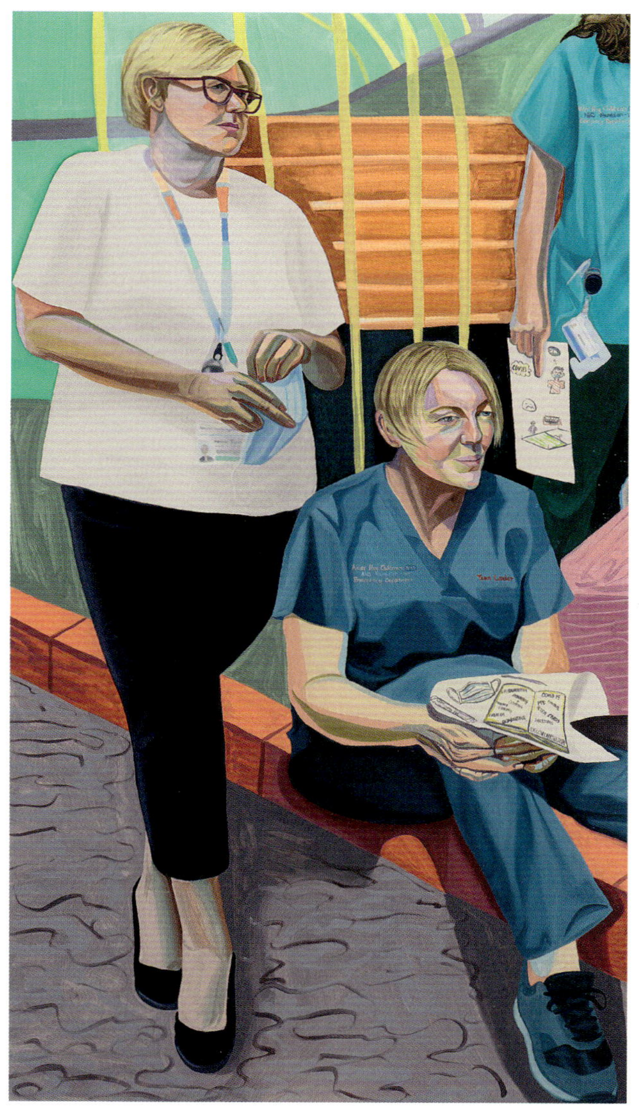

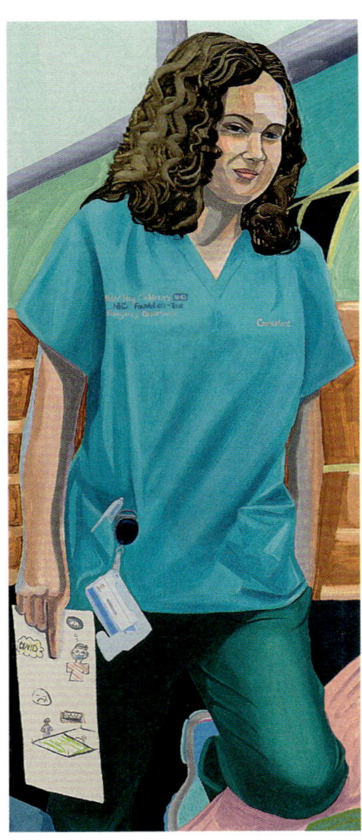

Charlotte

Consultant Physician

I'm a consultant paediatrician and I've been working at Alder Hey for nearly seven years. I work in the emergency department, so we see children with injuries or illnesses. With Covid, when it all started, we were worried that we were going to be overwhelmed with a huge number of patients, so we had to prepare for that. We sent out quite a lot of public health messages saying, 'If you don't need to come to hospital, please stay at home', which people did listen to. We initially went from a fairly normal, busy winter to sitting around with very few patients, which was really strange.

The biggest difficulty for us was the change in our policies and protocols; every day you would come in and something would have changed. It was quite emotionally exhausting trying to keep up with everything.

Another challenge is that we all wear the same blue scrubs and we have to wear a mask all the time, so it can actually be really difficult to recognise people. It's also been hard for the children. With the older ones you can explain why you're wearing a mask, but with some of the little ones, I've had a few who look absolutely terrified. You realise how much you usually use your facial expressions for communication.

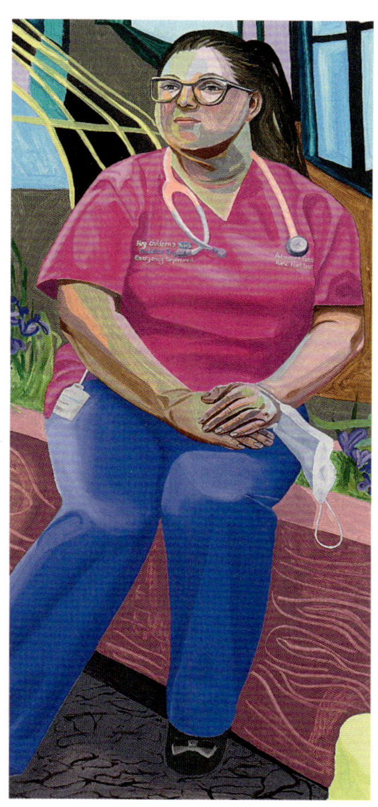

Leanne

Advanced Paediatric Nurse

I originally qualified as a nurse in 2001 and went straight into the A&E department at Whiston Hospital. After doing my master's degree, I moved to Alder Hey. I've been there for three years now.

My job is as an advanced paediatric nurse practitioner, so if you brought your child to A&E, you would either see a doctor or you'd see me. Parents trust you to look after their most precious thing; it's such a big responsibility. You're making massive decisions and ultimately parents trust that you've got the knowledge to make the clinical decisions. It's a lovely job, it can be stressful at times but it's very rewarding.

At the beginning of the Covid outbreak, I was going into work and myself and my colleagues were terrified of bringing something home to our loved ones. But we've adapted well because in A&E, we're trained in infection control and major incidents. My old boss once said to me, 'If you can work in A&E, you can work anywhere'. I think that's right, you have to adapt very quickly and be able to think on your feet.

Shirley

Consultant Physician

I'm a paediatric emergency medicine
consultant. Normally we would see
a variety of patients, from minor illnesses
or injuries, to very sick children with life
threatening conditions. Covid-19 has
changed my clinical role, physically,
emotionally and mentally. Children and
adults can carry the disease without
showing any symptoms and many of the
symptoms are common things we see
in children. So, I have to assume every
patient might have it. Essentially, you
think, 'This five-year-old could make me
seriously ill or even kill me'. Something
I'd never considered before.

School closure was the biggest challenge
in my personal life. As a key worker,
I was entitled to send my boys to school,
but we opted to keep them at home.
Home schooling was stressful, and
I tried to be unphased when I saw other
parents doing fun things with their
children during lockdown. I also self-
isolated at home for around a month and
a half to avoid potentially infecting my
family. This meant eating and sleeping
in a different room and wearing a mask
around the house. There were no hugs
or cuddles with my boys. There is also
the constant worry of not being able to
visit my family in Malta, if they became
unwell. Both of my siblings are in the
medical profession, so like myself, they
are at high risk of exposure.

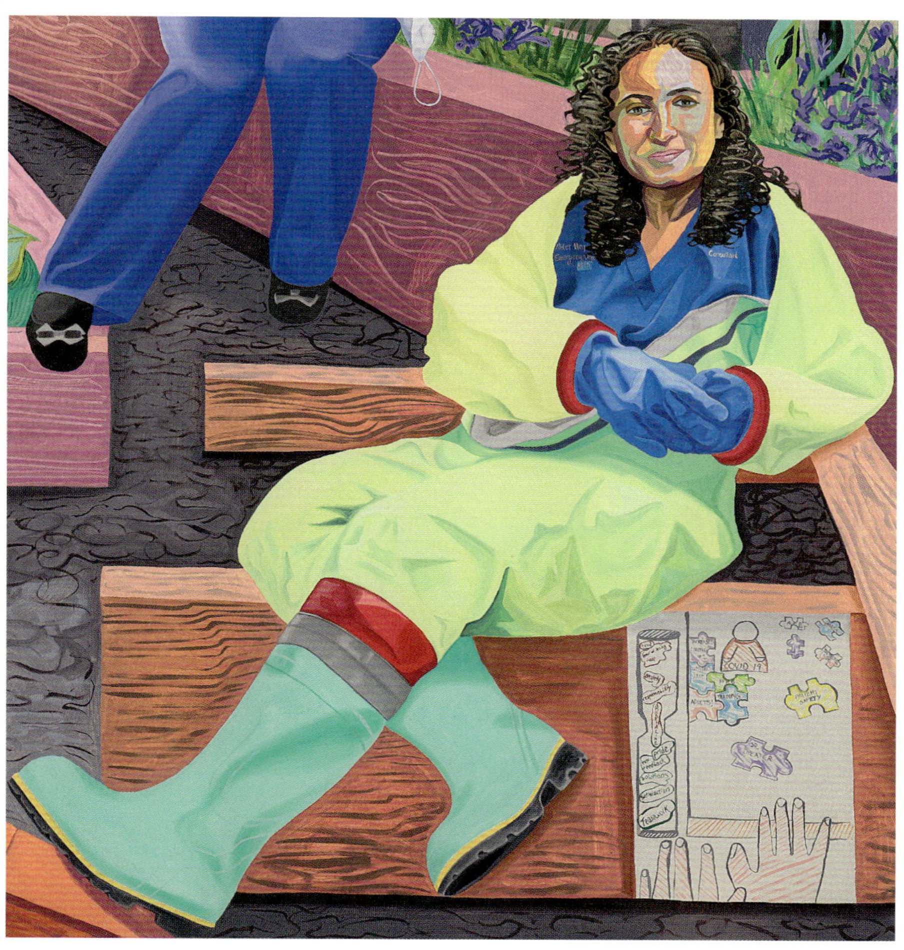
COVID 19
TRAINING
PATIENT SAFETY
responsibility
pride
feedback
solutions
satisfaction
Teamwork

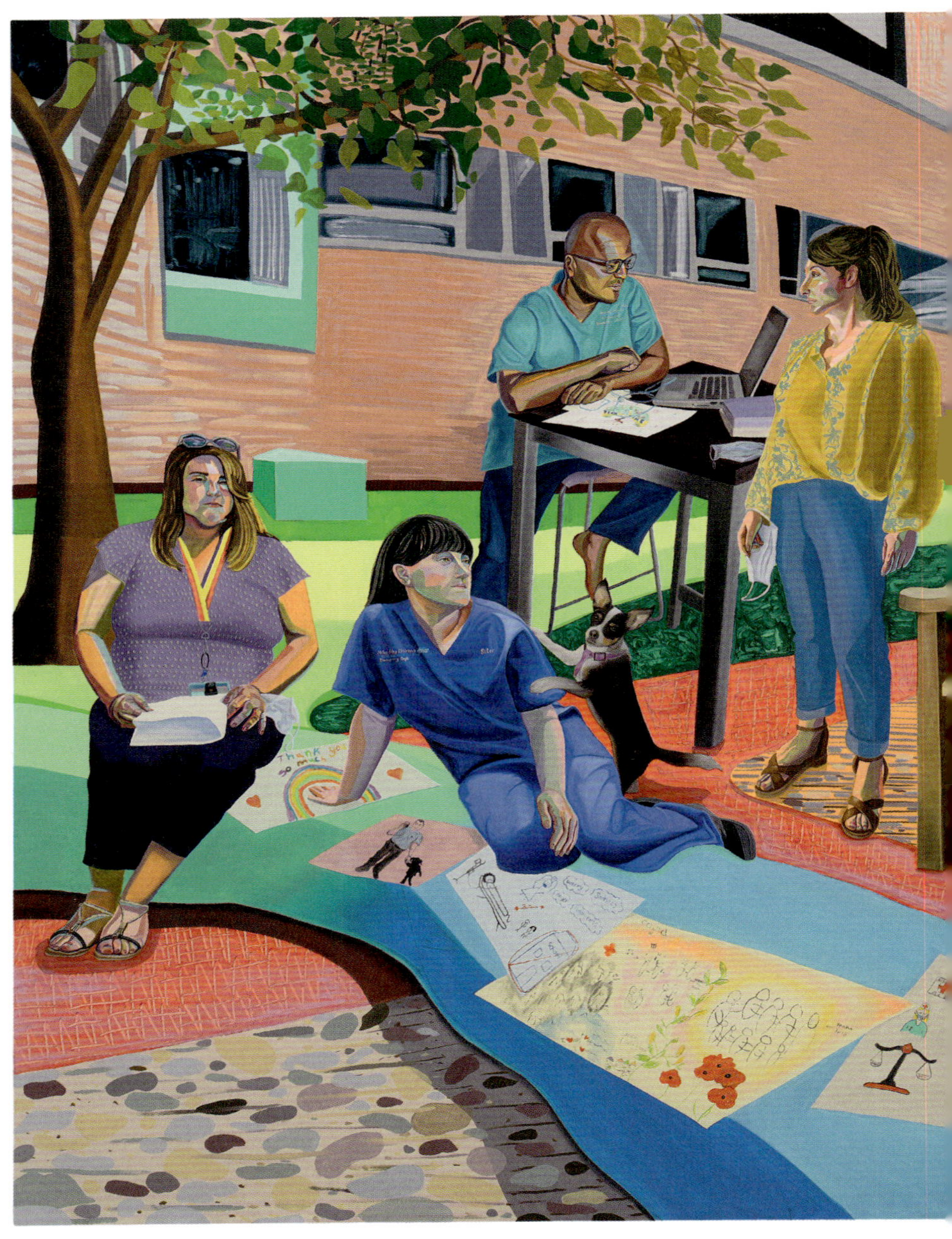

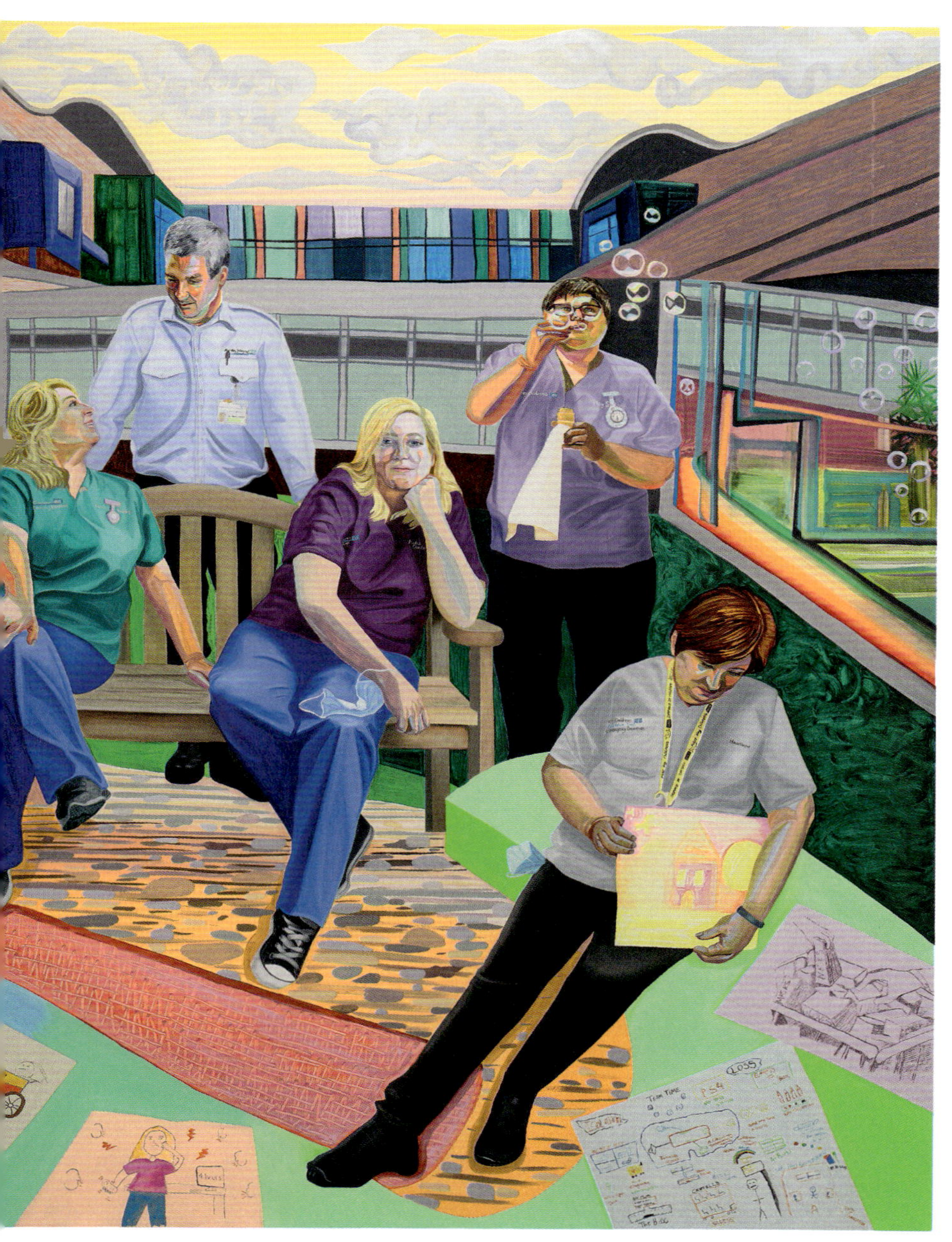

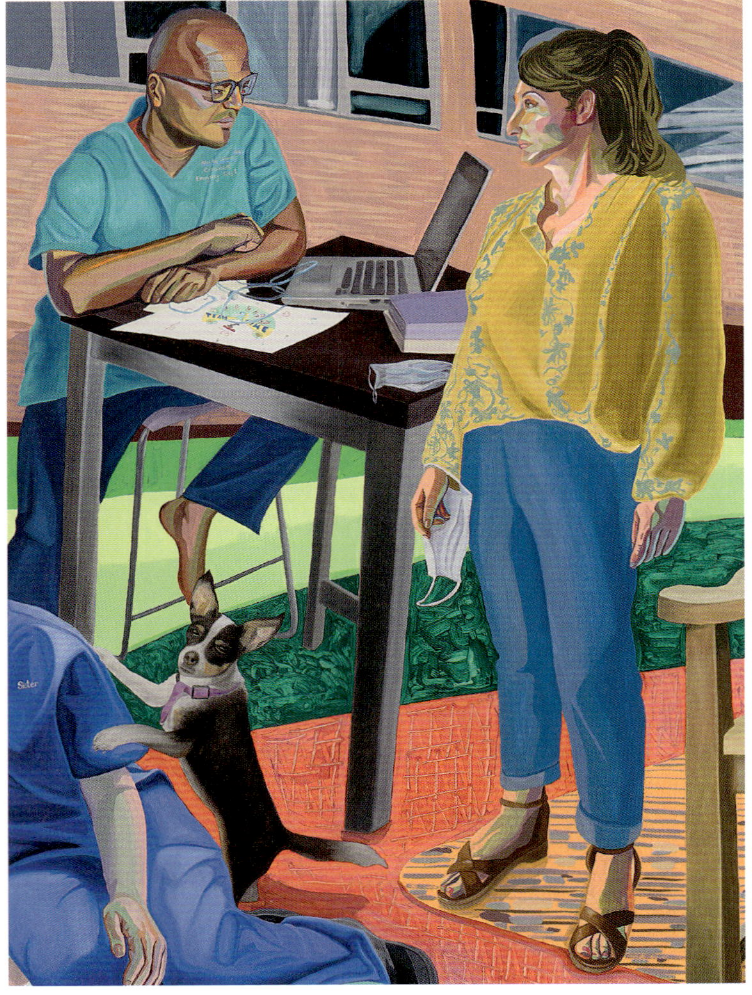

Lalith

Consultant Physician

I'm originally from Sri Lanka, but I was born and raised in Hong Kong and finished school in Beijing. What brought me to Merseyside was the Liverpool School of Tropical Medicine, where I did my master's degree in global child health.

Something we've seen during the pandemic is that Covid-19 has not physically affected children as severely as adults, but lockdown and social distancing have nevertheless been detrimental to children's physical and mental health. Closure of schools, restricted play and interaction with their peers, separation from extended family and socio-economic factors has impacted children and families on so many levels.

In the Children's Emergency Department, we have seen an increase of accidents in the home, delayed presentations of new diagnoses of serious illnesses, as well as heart-wrenching cases of child abuse and mental health issues.

I was put in charge of staff wellbeing when lockdown was first announced in late March. I wanted to pilot Team Time as part of our wellbeing strategy and it has given us a chance to share stories that aren't always heard from our porters and secretaries, as well as the doctors and nurses. Our team is very important to me, so I wanted to promote principles of psychological first aid and help my colleagues realise that they are not alone in how they feel.

Jo

Associate Director for Organisational Development and Consultant Psychologist

I'm a consultant clinical psychologist and my background is in child and adolescent mental health. I've been at Alder Hey Children's Hospital for almost fifteen years, and for the last three years I've been working in organisational psychology. This involves staff support and wellbeing – so anything to do with how it feels to work here. This has always been important, but during the Covid-19 pandemic it's become even more prominent.

When I came into this role the organisation had been going through a period of adversity. So I set up a staff advice and liaison service. This meant that staff members could talk to someone about their feelings and issues, either at work or at home. And we would either help directly or point people towards help. The need for this really accelerated once Covid hit. We have a drop-in facility in the hospital, so myself and my colleagues have been going in during the pandemic to continue running this.

Team Time sessions in the Emergency Department have been another key resource for staff wellbeing. This has provided a safe place for everyone in the department to be open with each other and has helped the team through some of their most challenging moments.

Sarah

Emergency Department Secretary and Team Leader

I'm a medical secretary; we're called 'pathway coordinators' at Alder Hey. We're the first point of contact for most patients and facilitate the pathway for patients' treatment and care.

The build-up to Covid was hard. China and Italy were really suffering but you'd think, 'It won't get that bad here', trying to stop yourself panicking. At work, we started getting constant emails about how we were preparing.

I was relieved when the schools closed. I really struggled sending my daughter in for the last couple of days because I didn't want to put her in danger. In mid-March I started working from home so I felt glad to be in a bubble with just myself and my family and my stress calmed down. But you don't want to speak to your family about Covid, because you want to shield them. Talking to colleagues helped because it gave me a chance to speak to people who felt the same way.

Jodie

Senior Paediatric Nurse

I'm one of the senior nurses at the hospital in the emergency department, so I help to manage the staff who work alongside the doctors and other nurses.

Covid has made it tricky to communicate with people because you have to wear face masks and it's really hard with children. They can't see us smiling and that's a massive part of communication. We haven't been able to give hugs to people, if there's a parent or family member that's upset, we can't offer them a hug, which is difficult.

Talking to other colleagues has been really nice, you talk about your experiences and realise that they feel the same. It makes you feel like you're not alone. The team are all really lovely, it's like a family.

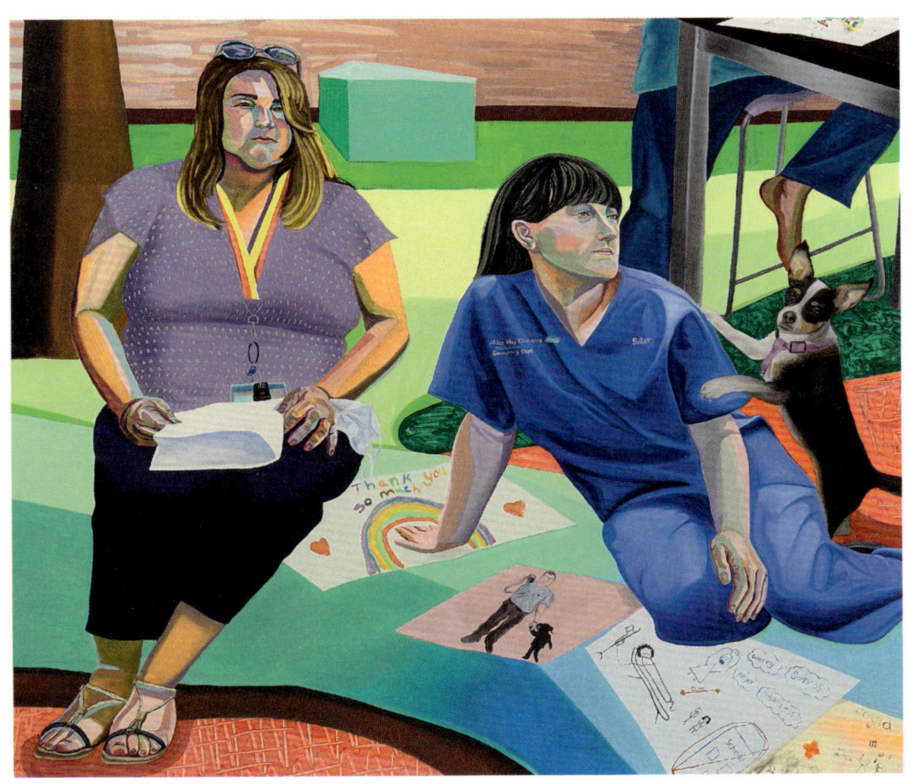

Thank you
so much
Saler

Claire

Healthcare Assistant

One of the good things during Covid is that we've got to spend lots of time with our children. We also got a new dog for our girls and I don't think that would have happened otherwise. But I have struggled with certain aspects and all the changes. We're front line workers, so we've worked all the way through. We also had to homeschool our children and my eldest daughter lost her job. I've tried my best but I still felt that it wasn't always good enough.

I work closely with the plastics team, dealing with facial injuries. That can be a very traumatic experience for the children. I've worked a lot with them, to help settle the children and learning what the best outcome is for certain injuries. Our team has become one big family and I think you really need to have each other's backs.

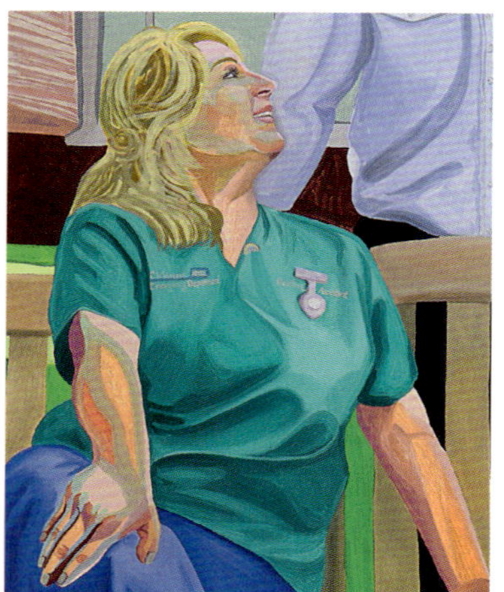

Kevin

Hospital Porter

I'm a porter at Alder Hey and my job is to transfer all the patients from department to department, ward to ward. Some of them are seriously injured, so we have to be very careful. We also move all the stock around the hospital. Sadly, children do die in A&E. This is especially hard for the young student nurses – they have never dealt with that – so I try to support them and tell them 'Don't feel ashamed, let the tears flow, don't bottle it up, when you go home, let it go.' When a child passes away, I go home and I raise a glass to them, that's my way of coping.

As a porter, one of our jobs is to take patients to the mortuary. When Covid-19 really started we had twelve adults in our hospital, which is very rare, but one of our ICUs was used for adults only. I took one of the patients to the mortuary and normally when a child passes away they are surrounded by their family, but in this case I was the only one accompanying them on their final journey which was very difficult.

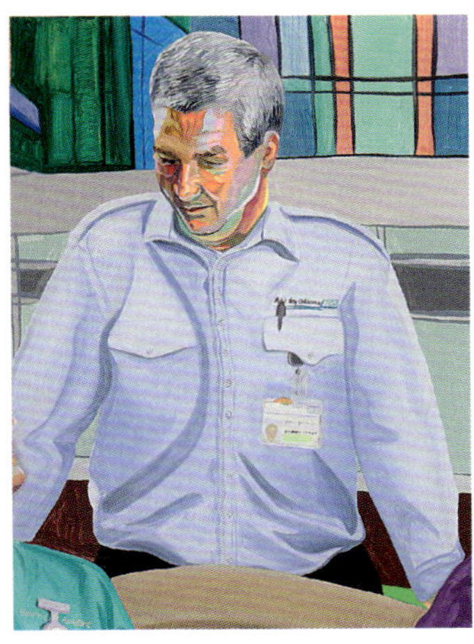

Leah

Clinical Practice Educator

I have a dual nursing role at Alder Hey. Sometimes I'm out in A&E looking after the children directly, but I'm also the clinical educator for the department, meaning I'm responsible for staff training and professional development. We see so many varieties of illnesses and injuries in A&E that we joke that 'accident and emergency' should stand for 'anything and everything'.

Covid has really changed things for us as a department. The number of patients dropped massively at the start of the outbreak. We were asking people to stay at home if they had Covid symptoms, but a lot of these symptoms are common childhood illnesses, so it's been difficult finding the balance between who should stay at home and who needs to be seen by a clinician.

The pandemic has drastically changed how we work together and the separation from family and friends has also been really difficult. We've felt isolated and separated from our normal lives, but thankfully we've had each other to keep ourselves going.

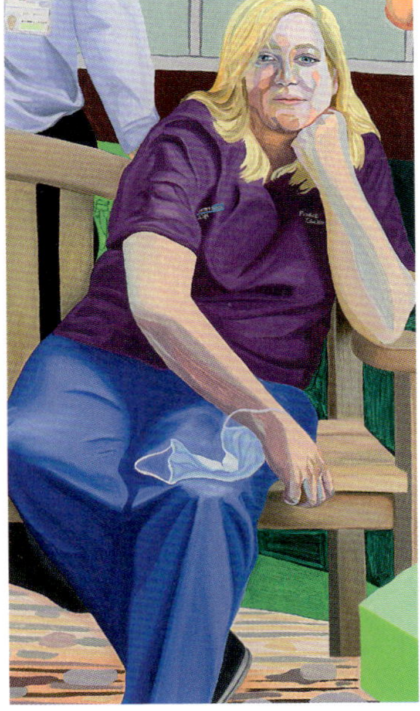

Rose

Health Play Specialist

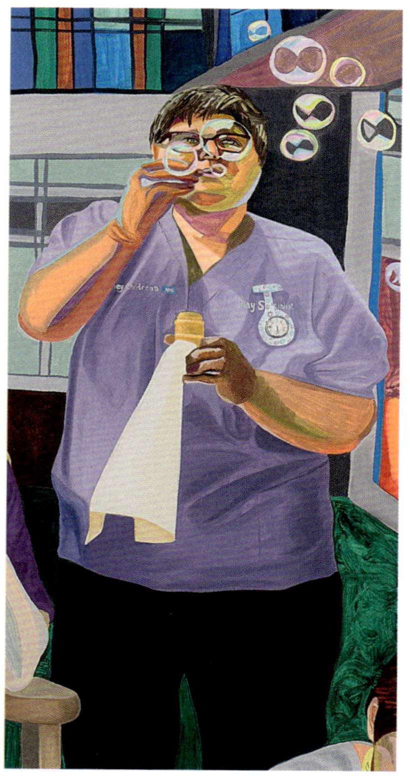

I was in hospital a lot as a child and when I was young hospitals could be very unfriendly for children. After working in a few other jobs, I did my degree and decided I'd like to work in a hospital. I wanted a better time for the children. Every day in A&E I paint with them. I have some paintings that they've done for me, that's when you know you've done something right, when a child gives you a picture.

I go to the operating theatre with the children and I also help keep them calm during invasive procedures like getting their blood taken. I have dreadful jokes that I tell. I'll say things like, 'What does Father Christmas do to his elves when they're naughty? He gives them the sack!' They are bad, but they do the job for eight-year-olds!

We always put out toys in the waiting areas but of course we had to remove everything when Covid hit. We had to take away the games consoles, the toy boxes were emptied, no books or crayons, absolutely everything went. We also had to wear face masks, which stopped me blowing bubbles for the children. That's a huge thing with the very young children who can be frightened just of having their temperature taken.

I socialise a lot with friends, I have them over to stay at my little house. That's something that's changed a lot. I didn't get my house until my late 50s, and it's been really important to me, it's got a nice little garden, friends come to stay. And all of a sudden it became quite a sad little house, because nobody could come to stay.

Sue

Housekeeper

I've been working in Alder Hey for nineteen years. I like the sound of the hustle and bustle, being on the go all the time.

At the start of lockdown it was so quiet as people were scared to come into A&E. The days felt so long, which made the situation worse, you felt like you were waiting for something really bad to happen.

I look after all the stock, and it's been a big responsibility looking after the PPE. It was daunting seeing colleagues get dressed up in their PPE. It reminds you that their lives are at risk. So I've got to make sure that they've got the right equipment to stay safe.

By the time I got home from work, I was mentally drained and physically drained. I was waking up with anxiety and my daughter was worried I was going to die, so that was upsetting. I'm not as anxious as I was and I try to focus on the good things, but it's in the back of your mind all the time. There was no way that I could work from home; I had to be on the forefront. But I am glad I'm part of it.

My brother has a serious illness affecting his immune system. I've been doing his shopping, putting it on his doorstep and talking to him from the gate. I like looking after people, it's in my nature, it's why I'm in the job.

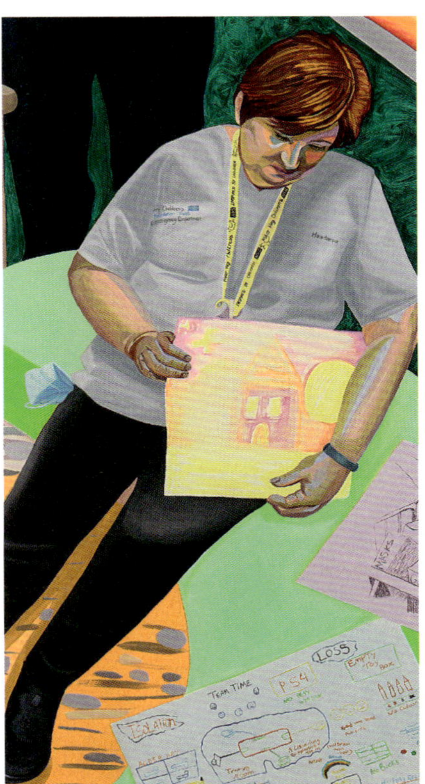

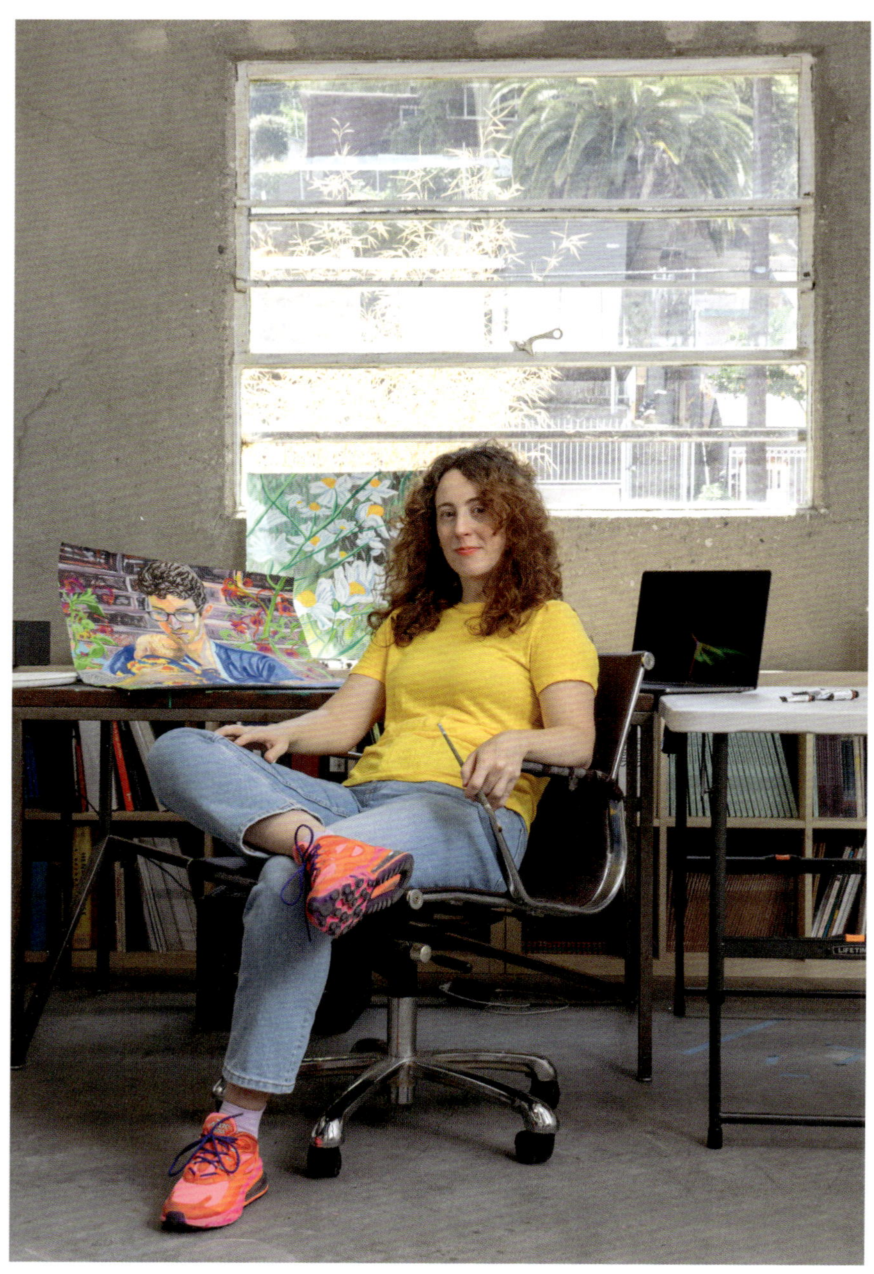

Aliza Nisenbaum in her studio

List of Works

All dimensions
are in mm

Agapanthus 2020
Watercolour on paper
762×559
p.21

Alan, Student Nurse 2020
Watercolour on paper
762×559
p.15

Ann, Nurse 2020
Watercolour on paper
762×559
p.41

California Poppy Field 2020
Watercolour on paper
762×559
p.42

***Calum, Professor of
Outbreak Medicine and
member of SAGE*** 2020
Watercolour on paper
762×559
p.31

Colin, Nursing Lecturer
2020
Watercolour on paper
559×762
pp.26–7

Datura 2020
Watercolour on paper
762×559
p.20

Emily, Critical Care Nurse
2020
Watercolour on paper
762×559
p.19

Jessica, Student Nurse 2020
Watercolour on paper
559×762
p.36

Naveena, Student Nurse
2020
Watercolour on paper
762×559
p.33

Night Bouquet 2020
Watercolour on paper
762×559
p.25

Poppy Blooms 2020
Watercolour on paper
762×559
p.37

***Reverend Jackie,
Hospital Chaplain*** 2020
Watercolour on paper
762×559
p.16

***Ryan, Respiratory Doctor
in Training*** 2020
Watercolour on paper
762×559
p.39

Shari, Intensive Care Nurse
2020
Watercolour on paper
559×762
p.28

Stephen, Orthoptist 2020
Watercolour on paper
762×559
p.23

Succulents 2020
Watercolour on paper
762×559
p.34

***Team Time Storytelling,
Alder Hey Children's
Hospital Emergency
Department, Covid
Pandemic*** 2020
Oil paint on canvas
2413×3810
pp.52–3

***Team Time Storytelling,
Steven Gerrard Garden,
Alder Hey Children's
Hospital Emergency
Department, Covid
Pandemic*** 2020
Oil paint on canvas
1905×2413
pp.44–5

MIX
Paper from
responsible sources
FSC
www.fsc.org
FSC® C004116